DVD INCLUDED

Understanding *Your Toddler*

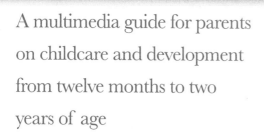

A multimedia guide for parents
on childcare and development
from twelve months to two
years of age

Mary Ann LoFrumento, M.D., F.A.A.P.

This book is dedicated to the memory of Dr. Bayard Coggeshall
who taught me the art of pediatrics and inspired me with
his practical wisdom and dedication to his patients.

Acknowledgments I would like to thank all the pediatricians at Franklin Pediatrics in New Jersey for their editorial assistance, especially Dr. Fern Gotfried, Dr. Julie Ashton, Dr. Maureen Baxley, Dr. Marisa Rosania, Dr. Joan Sorenson, and Dr. Wendy Lee for their review of the material. I would like to especially thank Dr. Baxley for her contribution to the sections on feeding and nutrition.

I am indebted to Gerri Perkins, IBCLA and President of TLC-The Lactation Connection (Florham Park, New Jersey), for her contributions to the section on breastfeeding toddlers. I am also grateful to Carolyn Varca for her help in updating the References and Resource Section and for her insights as a new mother.

I would like to thank my original editor Diane Dubrule for getting the book off the ground and my current editor Pamela J. Principe-Golgolab of PNA Associates Inc. for reorganizing and re-editing the book into its current form. Thank you also to Jen Conde at Franklyn Ideas for her work on the current layout. The creation of the DVDs would not have been possible without the hard work and expertise of my producer Dawn Gual.

I am also grateful to all my friends, neighbors and family members as well as the physicians, employees and patients of Franklin Pediatrics and the parents of the children at the Y's Owls Day Care Center of the Morris Center YMCA who allowed their babies to be photographed for this book. I am also appreciative to Ashley Kindberg, director of the Y's Owls, and her staff for all their help with this project.

And finally, I am grateful to my husband John for his long term support of this project and to my daughter Elizabeth for her valuable insight and advice.

By providing basic information on growth and development, nutrition and safety, we hope to give you the foundation on which you can build your knowledge through reading, lectures and other activities. This book and DVD is intended to complement, not substitute for your pediatrician or family practitioner. Any time you have concerns about your baby's health or development, please consult these experts.

About the Author

Mary Ann LoFrumento MD, F.A.A.P.

Born and raised in New York City, Dr. LoFrumento attended Barnard College and then the University of Pennsylvania where she received her medical degree. It was during her pediatric residency at Babies Hospital Columbia Presbyterian that she began writing simple outlines on childcare for parents. After moving to New Jersey, she started Franklin Pediatrics. For 17 years, she was the managing partner of this group, currently one of the largest pediatric groups in New Jersey caring for thousands of children. Immediately seeing a parent's need for accurate and easy to find information, she began expanding her outlines to include all aspects of childcare.

In 1996 she attended New York University and studied video production to pursue ways of enhancing her teaching materials. Shortly after that she founded HALO Productions and in 2002 Simply Parenting. Her unique approach to the production of multimedia products stems from more than two decades experience in clinical practice and medical education with a special interest in developmental and behavioral pediatrics.

Previously a Clinical Assistant Professor at Columbia University's College of Physicians and Surgeons, she is currently an attending physician at the Goryeb Children's Hospital of New Jersey and has remained active in teaching throughout the years. She conducts workshops for parents on all aspects of childcare.

She currently lives in New Jersey with her husband and daughter.

> "There is but one challenge greater than raising your child—trying to decipher all of the information that is out there."

–*Mary Ann LoFrumento, M.D., F.A.A.P.*
Founder, Simply Parenting

About Simply Parenting

When I opened my pediatric practice in 1985 and began seeing new parents and their babies, I was often asked for recommendations on books to read. As I worked to put a list together, I soon realized that there was a confusing amount of material that new parents would find on the bookstore shelves or in the handful of magazines devoted to babies and their care. In fact, as I began working with new parents, I realized that they were overwhelmed with information. Often times it was conflicting, coming from many sources including family members, books and the media. In addition, they were tired and under pressure with their new responsibilities and often did not have the time to read several books.

I decided to help them by putting together the essential information that they need to care for their new babies in an easy to read guide. The feedback was very favorable and patients constantly told me that these guidelines were all they needed for the basics.

Over the next 18 years, I revised and expanded *The Guide to Understanding Your Newborn* and provided my patients with the same easy to read guidelines on childcare from two months to five years of age. Whether a new baby came into a family through birth or adoption, just about everything a new parent needed to know was enclosed in these pages. Each provided brief descriptions of common concerns and problems. The recommendations were based on information from well-noted authorities like the American Academy of Pediatrics as well as insights from my two decades in private practice caring for thousands of patients.

Things are even more complicated for parents today. The bookstore shelves contain hundreds of books on childcare, there are several magazines dedicated to parenting and the "virtual bookshelf," the Internet, offers a seemingly endless stream of even more choices. Not only can you order books, videos and DVDs online, but also the Internet has provided new parents with access to hundreds of sites, each with their own version of important and useful information.

This incredible information overload can add greatly to the confusion experienced by parents and can leave them feeling quite bewildered and frustrated. And as childcare experts speak out on morning talk shows or the media points out one more thing that new parents have done "wrong," parents have lost confidence in their own judgment and abilities. They are frightened that they will harm their children if they do not listen to the "experts."

I feel new parents have plenty of confusion and what they need most is simplicity.

That is what *Simply Parenting* is all about. My goal is to "bring childcare back to the basics" and help you as a parent feel less anxious and more confident as you begin the most rewarding journey of your life.

Mary Ann LoFrumento, M.D., F.A.A.P.
Founder, Simply Parenting

How to Use This Book and DVD

This edition in the *Simply Parenting Childcare Series* focuses on the second year of life - twelve months to 24 months — commonly known as the "Toddler Years." Like all the books in the series, it is well organized and full of easy to find information. It contains just about everything that a parent needs to know during these years in a concise ready to use format. There are brief descriptions of common concerns and problems, combined with helpful, expert advice.

 Throughout this book look for the "camera" icon. This indicates that this information is visually highlighted on the DVD, which is included in the back of this book. DVD chapters are linked to the age and developmental level of your toddler. They provide a visual guide to normal development (The Two-Minute Baby) and illustrate the best play activities for each age group (Simply Playing.) (Behavior Basics) offers tips on handling some common toddler problems. We've also included a special section on keeping your toddler (Safe and Sound.) The DVDs are easy to navigate and designed so a parent can go directly to a specific section or watch the whole program.

As your baby grows, read or view each section a little before your child reaches that age. This way you will be prepared for your toddler's developmental changes and how you need to adapt to them. When you have a question, search for the information using the book index or scan the topics in the DVD menu.

To further assist parents, at the end of each book I have also included a *Reference and Resources Section* with reviews of books, videos and web sites, which through my experience, I feel are good quality sources of information with the least amount of advertisements.

Our web site www.simplyparenting.com offers brief articles about common problems and normal development right at your fingertips. It also provides links to some other well-respected sites.

Your Toddler

Your Toddler

"The fundamental job of a
toddler is to rule the universe."

–Lawrence Kutner, child psychologist and author.
Toddlers and Preschoolers, 1994

An Introduction to Understanding Your Toddler

It begins with the first steps. One day your baby decides it is time to walk. You grab the video camera. You clap and smile, and your baby knows this is something special. Everyone asks him to repeat this great feat. He obliges and enjoys the attention. A few months later he continues along in natural development and begins to climb on top of the kitchen table. You scream "No!" as he prepares to leap. You look horrified and your confused toddler does not understand why this next step in his development has not resulted in the same reaction as mere walking. His gaze asks – *"Where are the cameras?" "Where is the applause?"*

Welcome to Toddlerhood! This phase of your child's development begins when your baby starts to run, climb and explore his world, and suddenly, you must hold him back to avoid the real dangers that he is unaware of. It's a challenging time as he strives to become his own little person. As a parent it means helping him to do this in a safe protected environment and to begin to teach him the limits on his behavior.

From here on, your delight at your toddler's advancement in physical and mental development will be balanced against your fear that he will get hurt. All he knows is that he must move forward on this developmental road. Your toddler must begin to become an independent individual. And you must help him achieve this, *safely.*

Understanding your toddler's temperament is a very important first step. Your child's temperament will determine how easy or difficult it will be to guide her through this challenging time in her development.

The next step in parenthood is to learn to set limits on your toddler's behavior and to be able to tolerate your toddler's often angry reaction to your restrictions. This is the beginning of your child's education in civilized behavior, and you are the teachers. I cannot express how important this is to helping your child grow up to be a responsible member of society.

This guide to <u>Understanding Your Toddler</u> could also be called *How to Prepare for Your Child's Adolescence*. I know that stage of your child's life seems to be very distant in the future as you cuddle this soft innocent bundle. But this is where it all begins. If you wait until your child is older to set limits on his behavior, it will be much more difficult.

So there will be challenges in sleeping, feeding or getting dressed. You will experience tantrums, aggressive behavior, fears and often your toddler's utter frustration at a world he is trying to master.

Through it all, you will witness some incredible developmental milestones. Your toddler will begin to think, to solve problems, to communicate, to entertain and to become an individual. Your relationship will become richer despite the challenging times. In the end all she really needs is to know that you love her, that you understand her, and that you are there to help her and keep her safe. A good sense of humor and talking with those who have been there will help you appreciate this period in your child's life.

Enjoy your toddler!

Your toddler is a unique individual from the day he or she is born. This includes differences in feeding, sleeping patterns, personality and temperament. Therefore, no one method can be applied to all babies. And what is right for one baby and family may not be right for another.

Toddlers develop at different rates. Don't fall into the parent comparison trap! Even with siblings! Enjoy the differences.

Normal and loving stimulation is all that a toddler requires for growth and development. Playing, reading and speaking with your baby will do just as much for his or her intellectual growth as all products designed to stimulate rapid development. Think basic and simplicity when selecting toys. Avoid electronic toys and "educational" products.

Setting limits is essential for a toddler to develop self-control. As a parent you must remember that you are in charge and you must be able to tolerate your child's temporary anger towards you.

Family, friends and our culture will place tremendous pressure on you to conform. If you decide to do something just because of these pressures, and not because you really feel comfortable, you are not doing yourself or your infant any good.

Advertising for toddler products is carefully aimed at your insecurities. The message is that these products are essential to your child's health and well-being. The reality is that you can do without 90% of these products. Be a good consumer. Carefully examine products and their claims before purchasing and read unbiased comparisons before making decisions.

"Differences in temperament, even at the extremes,
are in the normal range of behavior.....Being alert
to temperamental differences and understanding
how they require different care-giving
approaches are crucial to nurturing children's
healthy emotional growth."

–Stella Chess, MD Temperaments of
Infants and Toddlers in J.R. Lally
(Ed) Infant/Toddler Caregiving (1990)

Temperament and Personality

Every baby, child and ultimately adult is unique. We
are a combination of innate traits, genetic material,
environmental influences and something called *tem-*
perament. All of this works together to form our
personality: who we are and how we interact with
the world and with those who share our world.

A group of researchers led by Dr. Stella Chess and
Dr. Alexander Thomas pioneered the study of
temperament and have followed a group of "babies"
from birth until middle age to see what traits continued
throughout a person's life. This fascinating study
demonstrated what some parents, doctors and nursery
nurses have always known. Babies are "born that way."
In addition, a person's temperament is not something
that can be changed. It is something that we need to
recognize and understand.

Why is temperament important?
Your child's temperament will affect everything that
you do (or try to do) with him. Moreover, you have
a temperament too. If your style is in contrast to your
child's, you may have difficulty managing common

behavior problems. If you have an understanding and appreciation for your child's temperament, as well as your own, the toddler years will be easier to navigate. This is true whether a baby is naturally born into your family and shares your own genetic traits or is adopted into your family.

What kind of temperament does your toddler have?
Every child's temperament is based on a number of traits. By observing the way your child reacts to certain situations, you can determine his or her temperament. There are books in our *Reference and Resources Section* and an excellent web site that will do an on-line profile to help you understand what type of temperament your child has. Here is a basic summary:

Sensitivity: How sensitive is your toddler to distractions or to small differences in the taste or texture of food, or the material or color of clothing, or the room environment, light, noise, or temperature?

Activity level: How much movement do you observe in your toddler during the day and during sleep?

Intensity: How intense are your toddler's reactions whether they are positive or negative?

Adaptability: How quickly does your toddler adapt to changes and transitions?

Approach or Withdrawal: Does your toddler approach or back away in new situations or from new people?

Frustration Tolerance: How easily does your toddler become frustrated with limits set on his/her activities or when confronted with obstacles?

Regularity: How predictable are your toddler's daily patterns of sleeping, eating and elimination?

Soothability: When your toddler is upset, how easily can she be calmed, soothed or even distracted by something else?

As you can see, if your toddler is easy going, can tolerate a high level of frustration, adapts well to change and has regular patterns of eating and sleeping, life is going to be smooth and easy. Conversely, if your toddler is very sensitive, has intense reactions, has a high level of energy, has irregular patterns of sleeping and eating or cannot tolerate frustration very well, life is going to be a bit more of a challenge.

Just as important as your child's temperament is your own. Opposing styles can cause unrealistic expectations in parents and be a great source of conflict and frustration. For example, the less active or shy "slow to warm up" child can be a challenge especially if he has parents who are high energy and love to interact with people.

Every stage of development comes with its own set of challenges and normal tasks that must be mastered. Temperament can soften or roughen these tasks. In order to better understand your child's temperament you may wish to check into some of the books or web sites in the *Reference and Resources Section*. In addition, if you are having difficulties or nothing you read here or elsewhere seems to work with your child, discuss her temperament with your pediatrician or family practitioner. Maybe getting a clearer understanding of both your child's temperament and your own can help.

"Give them just one tiny biscuit
and they will turn it into
10,000 teeny little crumbs."

Anonymous, internet reviewer
dooyou.co.uk

Feeding and Nutrition

**General
Guidelines**

Childhood obesity is rising at an alarming rate in our country and along with this rise is an increase in type II Diabetes in adolescents. Toddlerhood is the best time to begin encouraging healthy eating habits. Your responsibility as a parent is to offer healthy foods in a nurturing environment. Your child's job is to decide what and how much of what is offered he will eat. This is a very important concept and worth repeating to yourself from time to time.

In simplest terms - provide a balanced diet for your toddler, limiting sweets and salt. Limit milk consumption to 16-24 oz per day and undiluted juice to 4-6 oz per day. Avoid all carbonated beverages under the age of two years. Offer a variety of nutritious foods over time to your toddler and his nutritional needs will be met.

And although this advice may seem contrary to the concerns about obesity, the nutritional needs of babies and toddlers are different from those of adults. Do not restrict fat and cholesterol (contained in healthy food choices such as meats), which are necessary for adequate growth. Do not give babies and toddlers high fiber, low calorie foods, which may not have enough calories. It is the limitation of sugary foods with excess calories and limited nutrition that is most important at this age.

Milk

There is still some debate amongst the experts about whether it is best to use whole milk (3.5% fat) or low fat milk (1-2%). Skim milk is never recommended for toddlers. The debate centers on the need for fat for proper growth and the risk of fat for later heart disease and obesity. If you limit your child's consumption of milk to 16 oz per day it may not matter which milk you use (1%, 2% or 3.5%) since the percentage difference is small and the total amount of fat consumed is low.

Officially, the Academy of Pediatrics recommends whole milk (until age 2) although you may wish to discuss the choice of type of milk with your pediatrician, especially if your toddler is showing signs of excessive weight gain.

Calcium and Iron

The minerals to be most concerned about for toddlers are calcium and iron. Milk is the main source of calcium, and 16 - 24 oz. each day will provide most of the calcium a child needs after 12 months of age. If your child refuses milk, serve other food sources of calcium such as cheese, tofu, greens (collard, kale, mustard, spinach), broccoli and calcium supplemented orange juice, fruit juices, waffles, graham crackers and goldfish. If your child cannot take any dairy products try calcium fortified soy or rice milk. There are so many calcium-fortified foods now that other supplements are rarely necessary.

Iron-enriched cereals provide the first non-formula source of iron for children. As your child grows, red meat, fish and poultry will provide additional sources of iron. For children who do not eat (or refuse) meats, try substituting all types of beans, peanut butter, raisins, prune juice, sweet potatoes, spinach and egg yolks which are good sources of iron, especially if served with Vitamin C juice which helps iron to be absorbed more efficiently. Remember to limit the amount of juice, however, for too much can decrease your toddler's appetite for other foods.

**Common
Concerns**

Food Fights

Feeding is an area where parents and toddlers can get into major power struggles. If you are frequently worried that your child is not eating enough, or not eating the right kinds of foods, this anxiety may cause you to pressure your child, who immediately picks up the cue that this is an area for struggle. In battles over food, you, the parent almost certainly will lose. The more you force your child to eat, the more she will resist. If this leaves you feeling out of control – remember, *you are in control.* You control the food you offer your child. Eventually, she will get hungry and eat.

If toddlers are not given more than 24 oz. of milk and 4-6 oz. of juice per day, and are not given excessive sugary snacks between meals, they will eat an adequate amount of calories if offered a variety of nutritional foods. This is known as relying on "natural hunger" to achieve a balanced diet. Moreover, it may occur over several days of eating, not in one 24-hour period.

Eating the Same Food

It is normal for toddlers to want to eat the same food day after day. This will last a few weeks, and then the preference will change to a different food. As long as the food is not candy or other non-nutritious item, let your child eat the preferred food. Over time, he will get a variety of foods.

Playing With Food

It is also normal for toddlers to play with their food as they learn to feed themselves. This means mealtime is messy, with food on the face, hair, table and floor. She will resist your attempts to feed her. Despite your concerns about whether any food is finding its way to the tummy, let natural hunger help the process. If soft foods are being smeared, try more finger foods.

Not Eating Enough

Toddlers usually eat one good meal a day. If juice, milk and snacks are limited, and if a variety of foods is made available, he will consume adequate calories and nutrients over the course of several days.

Won't Eat at a Meal

If your toddler refuses to eat anything at all at a meal, give only water for the next two to three hours, then offer the meal again. Do not give snacks, milk or juice in the interim. This method is very effective in encouraging your child to eat. Natural hunger will solve most of these problems.

Prefers to Drink Milk

Do not give additional milk to make up for a meal. This is a common mistake parents make in their desire to get calories into a picky eater. Your active toddler will prefer to drink a meal rather than to sit down and have mealtime. However, drinking excessive amounts of milk will decrease his appetite and will not provide adequate nutrition. In addition, too much milk can lead to blood loss in the stool and iron deficiency anemia.

Will Not Eat Fruits or Vegetables

Usually, a toddler will eat a small amount of fruits or vegetables. Both contain similar vitamins and minerals. It's not necessary, and may be unrealistic to expect your toddler to eat all types of fruits and vegetables. Find the ones your child likes, and continue to offer new foods over time. Taste preferences change often—your child may refuse carrots now, but develop a liking for them in a week.

Breastfeeding

Many mothers and their babies choose to continue nursing beyond babyhood. The AAP recommends nursing for at least one year and as long after that as the mother and baby choose. The milk continues to be good for the nursing toddler and research shows significant health advantages which include fighting infection, delaying or preventing allergies, and delaying the development of eczema in children who have a family history. For example, studies have shown that middle ear infections are less severe for up to three years in the nursing child.

For many mothers, nursing a toddler helps them meet their baby's needs for closeness, security, and comfort. It is very easy to calm a tired, frustrated, or frightened toddler by a few minutes of nursing. Some mothers are concerned because they have heard that nursing beyond the first year of life will cause a toddler to have problems becoming more independent. Yet many psychologists observe that just the opposite may be true and these children may actually feel more secure, having had their early needs met.

Pressure to wean can come from husbands, mothers-in-law, friends, or the checker at the grocery store. As you may have noticed, people (including perfect strangers) feel free to tell mothers how to raise their children. If you wish to keep this as a private matter, you can either express your views back or you can adopt a policy of not telling others that you are still nursing.

If it is your husband pressuring you, you may need to try to find out if the problem is really the nursing or something else bothering him that he is blaming on nursing. Some husbands fear the child will never wean or that waiting to wean will make the process more traumatic. He may need reassurance that there is no magic age to wean and that all children wean when they are ready. He may feel that you are not available to him for intimacy while you are still nursing. If this is the case, a good heart to heart discussion and allowing some time for just the two of you may be necessary.

Here are some tips for nursing your toddler:

Biting: If your little one is teething there is the tendency to clamp down to ease the discomfort. Make sure your child has lots of opportunity to chew on inanimate things. When you see this beginning to happen while you are nursing be ready with a finger to deftly place between those gums before your breast gets in the way. As the toddler drifts off to sleep is the typical time this happens. Be very watchful toward the end of the nursing.

If the biting seems to be unrelated to teething take a look back at what has been happening in your toddler's life. Often when there was an incident such as when he bit you and you understandably cried out in pain, he may react by biting frequently when he nurses. One way to deal with this is to spend concentrated time with your toddler in physical ways: holding him skin to skin, stroking, giving massages, singing to him. Try to think of ways that soothe him through his senses. Talk to your toddler soothingly to try to get his cooperation in not biting. Toddlers understand a lot more than we give them credit for.

Acrobatic Nursing: Toddlers are notoriously active and this can happen even while you are nursing. Just like with meal times, setting limits on activity during nursing may be necessary. Some mothers curb the acrobatics by cuddling their toddler in a blanket, using a sling, tucking one of the toddlers arms under their arm, holding hands with their child and not nursing in public if it gets too hard. You can go to the car if you are out shopping or tell your child you will nurse later. Then offer "later" when it is more convenient.

Nighttime Nursing: You may feel that you are not getting enough rest because of your toddler's nursing at night. Many mothers talk to their toddlers and tell them they will only nurse when the sun shines or if they nurse to sleep that they won't nurse again until the sun shines again. It is okay to put limits on nursing as you do on every other aspect of your toddler's life.

"People who say they sleep like
a baby usually don't have one."

Leo J. Burke, author

Sleeping

> **Facts about sleep in toddlers:**
>
> • Most toddlers require between 12 and 13 hours of sleep in 24 hours
>
> • One to two naps per day are common
>
> • The morning nap will be dropped by 15 months to two-years-of-age
>
> • Nighttime awakenings occur several times a night after nine months of age
>
> • Nighttime awakenings are normal in all infants and adults
>
> • Nighttime associations are what our minds associate with falling asleep
>
> • Nighttime associations are needed to go back to sleep during nighttime awakenings

General Guidelines

Although good sleep habits should begin during infancy, it is not too late to teach your child to go to sleep by himself and to sleep through the night. There are two schools of thought on this issue. One group believes that babies and toddlers should share a room or bed with their parents (co-sleeping) and should never be allowed to cry themselves to sleep. This movement, led by Dr. William Sears, and outlined in his book, <u>Nighttime Parenting</u>, is in direct opposition to the belief that babies

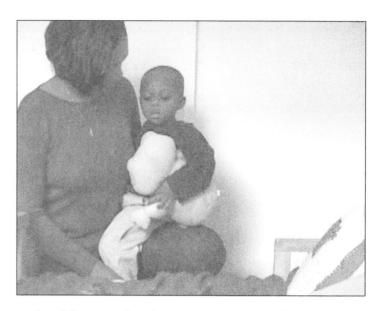

and toddlers need to learn how to go to sleep on their own. Dr. Richard Ferber was the first authority to write on this issue in his book, _Solve Your Child's Sleep Problem._ He outlines methods for training babies, toddlers and young children to sleep through the night.

Every parent must decide how he/she will raise their children. It should be noted that in both cases, your child will grow up fine. If you decide that your heart is more aligned with Dr. Sears and the idea of the "family bed," you must also accept that this is a long-term commitment. Your child may not sleep independently until he is four- or five-years-old.

If you decide that you are more aligned with Dr. Ferber and others and want to teach your child how to go to sleep without you, then you must be able to let your baby cry for a period of time during the training phase.

If you have made a personal choice to nurse your baby to sleep you may need to nurse your baby during the night as well. These are family decisions that should be discussed between you and your spouse.

Training Your Child to Sleep on His Own

Here is a summary of some key points for parents who have decided to let their infants and toddlers sleep by themselves:

- Set a regular bedtime and stick to it as much as possible

- Set a nighttime routine that is consistent and signals to your toddler that bedtime is coming

- Put your toddler to bed sleepy but awake

- Develop "Positive Sleep Associations" - comfortable room temperature and consistent lighting and noise

- Avoid "Negative Sleep Associations" - anything that requires your presence or that will not be present when your child wakes up in the middle of the night

  - Nursing or Bottle Feeding

  - Rocking to sleep

  - Music playing

  - Pacifiers (since they can not find them by themselves)

Create a Bedtime Routine

Toddlers depend on routines and rituals to understand their world, and bedtime rituals will help your toddler go to sleep. A ritual can consist of the reading of a favorite story after the bath, kissing all the stuffed animals, or singing a special song. This will become the signal for your child that bedtime has arrived and will also provide a transitional period during which he or she can prepare for the separation that sleep brings. It also gives toddlers some control of the situation since the ritual must be completed before they will go to bed.

Demystifying Crying It Out

Tell toddlers that it is time for sleep and let them fall asleep on their own. If a miracle occurs, the child will fall right asleep and sleep peacefully until morning. However, if a child has been used to having you there, a wail of crying in protest will most likely ensue. Several good books outline various methods for handling this next phase. Most experts believe that cold turkey "crying it out" is not good for either infant or parent.

Methods of checking in on your crying child have been developed. It is a good idea to consult one of the books or videos on sleeping and read more thoroughly about all of these methods. (Please refer to the *Reference and Resources Section* for some of these books.)

Many of the successful ones involve increasing the amount of time between these "checking in" points. When you enter the room, it is best to talk to your child in reassuring tones but to resist the urge to pick up your child. Tell him it is time for sleep and then leave despite the increased volume of crying. By the end of one week, your child should be sleeping through the night.

This is not easy to do and can cause a great deal of stress in any parent. If you are encountering difficulties, please discuss this with your pediatrician or family practitioner. It is also a good idea to make sure that your infant is well and not in pain from teething or an ear infection before you begin any program.

**Common
Concerns
About
Sleeping**

Jumping Out of the Crib

Toddlers are little acrobats and can surprise us by leaping or "falling" out of their cribs in an effort to get out of sleeping. Preventing injuries is the first concern, so you must create a safe sleep area. If you think it is time for a bed, you can make the switch earlier than two years. However, if you keep the crib, it is a good idea to lower the mattress and remove all bumpers or toys that can be used as climbing tools.

Make sure that the area around the crib or bed has a thick rug or small mattress in case your child can get out of the crib. If you make the switch to a bed, put a gate on the door to the room so that he cannot wander around the house (or easily get to your bed.)

Either way, if your child gets out of her crib or bed, simply take her back and say, "It's night time now. We go to sleep." Keep it simple and not playful. Say the words in a dull monotone. Do not cheer this new skill if she is climbing out of her crib. You may have to do this several times in a row, but she will get the message that she is not going to get what she wants and will probably give up if this is followed consistently. It is boring to hear the same thing over and over again.

Vomiting in the Crib

Another thing that may happen is that your child will cry and then vomit in the crib. If this happens, go in, silently change the child and bedding, and then follow the advice outlined above. "It's nighttime now. We go to sleep." He will get the message if you are firm, consistent and very dull!

Nightmares and Night Terrors

Nightmares are common at this age but are still frightening for your child. They usually occur in the early morning hours or after your child has been asleep for several hours. Comfort your child and reassure her that you are there to protect her. She will react in a way that shows you that she is awake and aware of you. **Never** let a scared child "cry it out." Stay with her until sleep returns.

Night terrors are very different from nightmares. They typically occur about one to two hours after falling asleep. They are actually a form of sleepwalking. Your child will appear awake but is actually in a deep sleep state. Usually, the child will suddenly begin screaming and appear absolutely terrified. His eyes will be open and he may even stand up. However, he does not respond to your attempts to comfort him. He may act as if you are not there or even try to push you away. Night terrors last about five to 15 minutes and, after a sudden yawn or sigh, your child will sink back into sleep. There is no recollection of the event in the morning. If these episodes recur, it is usually at about the same time each night. Despite the frightening appearance for observers, night terrors are harmless and are not a sign of serious trouble.

If you are having difficulties with nightmares or you suspect night terrors, please discuss this with your pediatrician orfamily practitioner. There are treatments available for both nighttime occurrences.

Bedtime Struggles in the Older Toddler

Here are some tips to help alleviate the struggles associated with bedtime:

- Keep the bedtime routine short (no longer than half an hour) and simple. For example, after the bath - read up to three stories, sing one song, say goodnight to the favorite stuffed animals, say goodnight to your child, then it's lights out.

- You should make it clear to your child (who is no longer in a restrictive crib and can open doors) that you mean business. If he keeps coming out of the bedroom, he should be returned as many times as necessary.

- Use a reward system for staying in bed. You cannot force your child to go to sleep, but you can force her into a bedtime. What she does in bed after that time is up to her. This may take a lot of work in the beginning, but it will pay off later.

- The alternative to this method is staying with your child until he falls asleep. If your child becomes used to this, or if the child has been sleeping with you, the transition to sleeping alone may be more difficult. Most children should be able to go to sleep on their own by age three, even if they have been raised in the family bed.

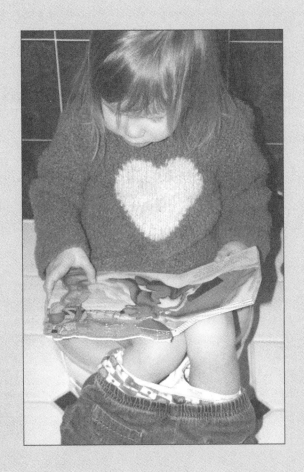

"The vitreous monster with it's yawning jaws

does not invite friendship or confidence at this age ..

It swallows up objects with a mighty roar,

causes them to disappear in it's secret depths,

then rises again thirstily for it's next victim

which might be-just anyone."

Selma H. Fraiberg   The Magic Years. 1959

Toilet Training

General Guidelines

Some children show readiness for toilet training between 18 and 24 months. This should not be confused with the achievement of toilet training, which may not occur until the child is between two-and-a-half to four-years-of-age. You may already have a potty in the bathroom and you both may have names for urine and stools. Your toddler may let you know he is dirty or wet, indicating a desire to have his diaper changed. Toilet training requires a combination of physical and mental developmental skills, which must be mastered before training can be successful. Here are some tips to get you and your toddler started:

How Do I Know if My Child Is Ready?

Your child should be able to walk well and be able to climb up and down from the potty unassisted. Your child must also be able to recognize when he has the urge to urinate or defecate. Your child then must be able to verbalize that urge. These are called "signaling abilities."

Other signs of readiness include dry nap periods, grunting or straining after meals, asking to have diapers changed after a bowel movement, or telling you she has had a bowel movement. This is a sign that she can recognize the signals.

What Do I Do Next?
You should buy a small potty or a potty seat that fits over your regular toilet and begin to discuss the topic with your child. You should begin using simple words (such as "pee-pee," "wee-wee" and "poop") to describe what is happening. Have your child sit on the potty in his diapers or clothes to feel comfortable. Remember — this is the early stage of training. Avoid putting pressure on your child before he is ready.

When Is a Bad Time to Start?
Try not to start toilet training during any type of upheaval in the child's world - for example, the move to a new home, the birth of a new baby, divorce or illness.

When is a Good Time to Start?
Remember, toilet training requires a combination of physical and mental developmental skills, which must be acquired before training can be successful. Your child must have the physical ability to hold urine and stool and must be able to recognize the urge to go. He

should be able to pull his pants down and sit on the potty by himself. He should be able to verbalize when he needs to use the potty.

Many children are ready for training by two-and-a-half-years-of-age. Some children will be ready a little earlier, some a little later. Boys typically train later than girls, although there are exceptions. You are the best judge of your child's readiness for toilet training.

It is important to understand that there is no innate instinct, which leads a child to toilet training. The desire to please parents is the driving force. Along with this is the desire to join the "big kids" and ultimately adult world. If there are disturbances within the child, disruptions in the family, or disruptions in the parent/child relationship, there may be problems with toilet training. Please discuss your concerns with your pediatrician or family practitioner.

How to Toilet Train

My Child is Ready. Now What Do I Do?
Dr. T. Berry Brazelton introduced a method in the 1960s that gradually introduces a child to the new idea of using a "potty." This remains a very successful method of toilet training with a "child-oriented" approach.

Have your child sit on the potty at a regular time of the day, every day, in all her clothes. This avoids the "cold seat" being a negative influence until the child gets used to all of this. Sit with the child and read a story or have a cookie. Your child should be free to leave at any time and should not be forced to sit on the potty.

After a week or so, the child should be taken with their clothes off to sit on the potty. No attempt should be made to "catch" urine or stool. This should be a pleasant experience with no pressure.

When interest in sitting on the potty is achieved, take your child to the potty for a second time during the day. This can be after a bowel movement has occurred, so he can be changed. Drop the stool into the potty and point out to him that this is the eventual plan.

When some understanding is noted and you sense a wish to comply such as a verbal expression telling you she has "to go," begin taking your child to the potty several times a day at regular intervals. Try to approximate the time when the bowel movements usually occur. Try to "catch" the urine or stool. Continue this as long as your child is willing.

As interest grows and your child realizes that you are pleased whenever she performs in the potty, you can begin experimenting with no diapers for short periods of time. During this time, your child's ability to go to the potty is pointed out and attempts to go should be rewarded with hugs, smiles and expressions of pride. At the same time, avoid too much praise, as this may make your child nervous about failure.

Your child should be encouraged to use the potty on his own. As training progresses and your child gains confidence, let him watch how to empty the potty into the toilet and flush. At this point, training pants such as diaper Pull-Ups or equivalent can be introduced and your child can be taught how to pull these up and down. There should be no pressure on the child to graduate to underwear before he is ready.

Books and videos about this topic are helpful, but always remember to read the book or watch the tape first so you are familiar with the contents. Make sure the method demonstrated is compatible with your own ideas and appropriate for your child's developmental level. And never just put a video on and not explain things to your child - they can get some pretty wild ideas about this subject! (Please see the *Reference and Resources Section* for some suggestions on this topic.)

Your child may still require diapers or Pull-Ups for nighttime and naps until training is fully achieved. Up to the age of four, accidents during sleep are normal and are not uncommon for several years after that.

If all goes smoothly, toilet training should take a few weeks to complete. If your child shows signs of stress, stop the training for a few weeks and then start over. Your child should never be punished or made to feel bad for failures in potty training. Accidents should be handled calmly and sympathetically. Your child should never be made to feel ashamed.

Common Concerns about Toilet Training

For a quicker method, which utilizes behavior modification techniques over a concentrated period of time, read <u>Toilet Training in Less Than a Day</u> by Nathan Azrin and Richard M. Foxx. If you have questions or concerns regarding toilet training, please let your pediatrician or family practitioner know.

Special Help for Boys

For boys, it is best to teach bowel training and sitting on the potty to urinate before teaching how to stand and urinate. The excitement of standing may inhibit the sit-down training. Standing for urination is most easily learned by observing older boys. Siblings or cousins also are great for this purpose because they love to show-off. Have your child aim at a piece of toilet paper or "toilet targets" to avoid a mess!

Stool Withholding

Although this is more of a problem in the preschool child, some older toddlers will begin to hold stool back if they do not wish to use the potty or if they have experienced a painful bowel movement. Always keep in mind that a child does not know that he "must" pass his stools. He does not understand the relationship between eating and "pooping." In his mind, if it hurts or if "I don't want to put this in the potty," he just won't. And he won't understand the connection with the stomach pains and discomfit that will follow days of withholding.

So if this happens, it is a good idea to discuss treatment options with your pediatrician or family practitioner as soon as it begins. Most doctors will recommend some combination of mineral oil or natural laxative to help keep the stools soft and break the cycle of pain and withholding. It may even be necessary to go back to Pull-Ups temporarily.

Bedwetting

Daytime and nighttime dryness are two different achievements. Bedwetting is "normal" for toddlers learning how to toilet train. And depending on the family history, bedwetting may last for years after daytime training is complete. If a toddler is having trouble staying dry, put them in Pull-Ups for bed and don't make a big deal about the issue. It is beyond your child's control.

"Never underestimate the abilities
of your child. The consequences can be tragic."

Dr. Mary Ann LoFrumento

Safety

**General
Guidelines**

DVD Chap 4

Toddlerhood is the most dangerous time for your young child. Increased mobility and fine motor skills coupled with a normal desire to explore everything means that your house must be fully childproofed by now. Your active and mobile toddler requires a high degree of supervision. He should never be left unattended, except when sleeping in his crib.

A special note on safety from Dr. Mary Ann:

In my two decades of experience as a pediatrician several toddlers died from preventable accidents at the hospitals that I worked in. They died in the following ways: a toddler drowned in a bucket of cleaning water, another choked to death when his pacifier on a string caught on a nail, another died by hanging from loose window blind cords, another died from carbon monoxide poisoning, one drowned in a swimming pool, another fell and died from an open window, and one toddler choked to death from a small toy lodged in the throat.

I have also cared for children who had the following injuries: a boy burned severely (needing skin grafts) from a hot cup of tea, a girl whose mouth was disfigured from biting into an electrical cord, several children who fell down flights of stairs, a boy who choked on a peanut and had to have part of his lung removed from the destruction peanut oil can cause, a boy who scarred his esophagus from drinking lye containing cleaning fluids, and many children who swallowed adult medications.

These events are heartbreaking – but more importantly - preventable.

Please follow the Blueprint for Safety!

Always remember the following:

• LEARN CPR

• The most important safety tip -
  Never leave a toddler unsupervised.

• Always use a car seat or approved booster seat.
  Never a lap belt.

• Make sure smoke detectors are installed
  and working.

• Install carbon monoxide detectors as well.
  It is the silent killer.

• Bathrooms and kitchens, in general, should be off
  limits unless supervised. These are the most
  dangerous rooms in the house.

• Be extra vigilant at other people's homes
  (especially if they do not have children.)

• Use safety latches, locks, and plug covers to
  childproof your home. (Buy safety kits that have
  everything that you need.)

• Make sure any childcare provider (even
  grandparents) follow these same guidelines.

Preventing Burns and Scalds

- If you have not already done so, set the water heater thermostat to 120° to avoid accidental injuries in the tub or sink.

- Pots and pans on the stove should have handles turned in-ward. Keep hot liquids out of reach during meal preparation.

- Be aware of hot liquids on a placemat or tablecloth, which your child might pull down.

- Never carry your child and hot liquids at the same time.

Preventing Choking

- **Do not** let children of any age chew on balloons.

- Cut all food into small pieces. Avoid round shapes that can easily block a child's airway.

- Avoid nuts (be extra careful at parties.)

- Avoid jewelry around the neck or hoop earrings, which can become loose, pulled off and easily swallowed.

Preventing Drowning

- Toilet bowl covers should have locks.

- Swimming pools should be fenced, with gates locked.

- Jacuzzis and hot tubs should be covered and locked.

- Buckets with water or cleaning fluids should be out of reach.

Preventing Electrical Shock
- Outlets must be plugged and electrical cords covered.

- Never allow a child to play with or put his/her mouth on an electrical cord.

Preventing Falls and Injuries
- Gates should be in place at the top and bottom of stairs.

- Windows should be locked and never left open if a toddler is in a room.

- Window guards should be placed on windows above the first floor (and are required in apartment buildings in many cities.)

- Sharp edges on tables and cabinets should be protected with soft strips of rubber. (Available in most safety kits.)

- Bicycle helmets should be worn even by children riding on tricycles.

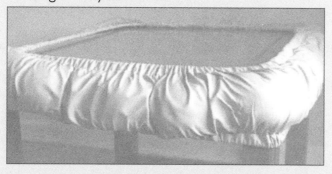

Preventing Gunshot Wounds
- Do not keep guns in the house.

- If you keep guns, keep them in a locked cabinet.

- Keep the ammunition in a separate locked storage space.

- Make sure all guns have approved safety locks.

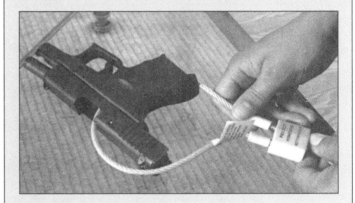

Preventing Hanging
- Window blind cords must be tied out of reach.

- Never keep these cords in the shape of a loop or "noose." Cut them into two cords.

- Cut all cords out of jackets and hoods.

• Always look around a room for any string or rope that could end up around a toddler's neck.

Preventing Ingestion and Poisoning

• Write the poison control number near all phones in the house (and program that number into your cell phone.)

• Dangerous cleaning materials and medicines should be high, well out of reach and latched shut.

• Be extra careful when visiting relatives ("purse poisons" are pills in Grandma's purse without child safety top.)

Preventing Suffocation

• Tie all plastic bags into a knot before disposing of them.

• Never let a child play with a plastic bag.

Preventing Strangulation

- **Never** tie anything around a toddler's neck, including necklaces or pacifiers.

- Cut all cords out of jackets and hoods.

Important Safety Facts

- Mouthwash is 25% alcohol and can cause convulsions if ingested by small children.

- Adult vitamins with iron or pain relievers such as aspirin or acetaminophen can cause death in a child who ingests a large quantity.

- The insertion of a metal fork into an electric outlet can kill a child.

- An electrical burn in the mouth of a child who has bitten a live wire can result in massive blood loss and disfigurement.

- Children can drown in bathtubs, toilets, buckets of water and hot tubs as well as swimming pools and lakes. It only takes a few short moments.

- Balloons are the leading cause of suffocation death in children.

- Twenty-seven percent of deaths by firearms in children under 12 were unintentional shootings.

Note: The Academy of Pediatrics no longer recommends the use of syrup of ipecac after an ingestion or poisoning. Discard any bottles you may still have at home.

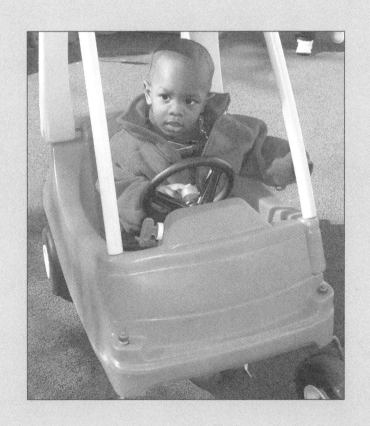

"I often think about the opening words of Charles Dickens'
A Tale of Two Cities: 'It was the best of times, it was the
worst of times.' I know Dickens wasn't talking about one-
to three-year-olds, but his words do capture the extremes
of emotion that toddlers and their parents experience every day.
Can there be a creature on earth as adorable — and as
trying — as a toddler?"

*Anne Cassidy, US writer. Don't Let Your Good Baby
Turn into a Terrible Toddler! Working Mother (November 1990.)*

Managing Toddler Behavior

All discussions on toddler behavior involve some form
of limit setting. It is very important to begin setting
these limits with your toddler for this is the beginning of
your child's education in civilized behavior, and as
parents, you are the teachers. To do this well you must
be able to tolerate the temporary anger of your child
towards you. A toddler's behavior will be "out of
control" because he does not have the innate ability to
control his actions. The development of "self-control" is
part of a learning process, which you and all of your
child's caregivers are at the helm of.

The following are some overall principles for managing
behavior and setting limits during this challenging time.

Routines are Very Important for Your Toddler
Toddlers need a certain order in their lives and they
depend on routines and rituals to help them understand
their world. Remember that toddlers are just becoming
aware of the rhythm of day and night. They cannot tell
time, however, and they certainly don't know what day
of the week or month it is. For some children, who

have difficulty making transitions, a chaotic day can be overwhelming, especially if they do not know what will come next. Parents can use this need for routines to their own advantage. Bedtime rituals, for example, will help your toddler go to sleep. Routines around mealtime, like setting the table with your toddler, will signal that a meal is coming. A ritual or routine gets your toddler involved in the activity, thereby giving her a feeling of control. Cooperation is more likely when this happens.

Create an Environment as Frustration-free as Possible

DVD Chap 3

Safe-proof rooms so your toddler can explore without a litany of "NO's!" from you. As much as possible, avoid situations that require long periods of good behavior and restraint. Remove temptation (the kitchen garbage can, for example) whenever possible to create a more peaceful atmosphere for everyone.

Be Creative

Use distraction and substitution whenever possible. Try to anticipate problems especially when visiting other people's homes.

Setting Limits is Essential

As I've discussed, children this age are driven internally. They do not have the ability to exercise self-control nor are they able to control their impulses. The main principle of discipline at this age means setting limits. By doing this, you are teaching your child self-control. Be patient - this takes time and, as with any new skill, it progresses through stages.

Take, for example, trying to get your child not to touch the electrical outlet. First, you say "no" and remove the child from the outlet. This is repeated 60 to 100 times. During the next phase, you will find your toddler at the outlet, but he is saying "no" as he touches it – an

indication that he is beginning to understand. The final phase is the internalization of the meaning of your "no," which gives the child the strength to fight the impulse to touch the outlet. At this point, he may think about doing it, but will not.

DVD Chap 10

Discipline and Time-Out

Discipline works when it is consistent among all childcare providers and when it is not harsh. Research has shown that it is the consistency, not the severity that is effective. The child's biggest fear at this age is losing his parent's approval. Your facial expression showing disapproval is a very powerful disciplinary tool.

By 18 months of age, children begin to understand consequences so an early form of "time-out" can be used. This is the unemotional, temporary shunning of the child for a period of about a minute and a half (or about a minute per year of age.) This can be accomplished by turning your back, walking away, or ideally by placing the child in a chair, bottom step or playpen (with no toys.)

Although an occasional smack on the behind will not be harmful to your child, spanking or hitting as a regular form of discipline could impair your child's ability to learn self control. It loses its effect quickly and it allows the child to pay the price for the crime without developing the internal controls that come from feeling remorseful. It also may reinforce the idea that hitting is an acceptable response when you are angry, especially if you are bigger.

Attacks on your child's self-esteem are worse than hitting your child physically. Be careful not to attack your child's sense of self-worth with statements such as "you're no good" or "you're a bad boy." Remember — it is the action that you disapprove of, not your child.

Any discipline, which is punitive, restrictive or coercive only teaches anger and rebellion. This can have the opposite of the desired effect by causing an increase in difficult behavior or temper tantrums. Also useless at this age are long speeches and attempts at rationalization. Your child will not understand what you are saying and it may give her more attention, there by rewarding the behavior.

Five Words or Less

When your toddler does something wrong, such as hitting, biting, throwing objects, let him know this is unacceptable. Grab both arms, put your face close to his and say in five words or less, "You do not hit!" or "No biting!" Then quickly, and without any other words, place him in a time out.

Time-Out

DVD Chap 10

"Time-out" is the most effective method of discipline for young children. It has been researched extensively and is used by hundreds of day care centers and nursery schools. It is simple to carry out and allows both parent and child to cool off.

How to Properly Use Time-Out

- Establish a time-out space in one particular room—the room where you spend the most time together is best. Use a chair, a step, or a playpen without toys. You can also create a time-out space wherever or whenever it is necessary. However, never put a toddler in a closed room or closet.

- The recommended length of "time-out" is one minute for each year of age. A timer can be very helpful.

- Establish what behaviors will result in time-out ahead of time. Have a "parent" meeting to decide what behaviors you wish to change. Never try to change more than two at a time.

- Be consistent. That means each parent and childcare provider is consistent.

- Remember the rule of using five words or less to tell your child what behavior you are putting them in time out for. Following the inappropriate behavior, say for example, "No hitting!" firmly and, without raising your voice and without further discussion, place the child in time-out.

- If your child will not sit in the chair, hold him in it from behind the chair putting gentle pressure on the shoulders. For an older child, resetting the timer teaches him to sit until told to get up. The key to success is to not say a word or look at the child during this time. Toddlers cannot stand being shunned.

- Following a time-out, do not bring up the incident again. Do not lecture and do not reprimand. Doing so has been shown to act as a positive reinforcement for the unwanted behavior by giving the child attention and could negate your disciplinary efforts. Equally unhelpful is any attempt to assuage your "guilt" by giving extra hugs and kisses to show your child that you still love him. Love is demonstrated in many ways and helping your child learn to control his behavior is one of them.

- The child should start with a clean slate after each time-out and should receive praise for the next positive behavior.

- Time-out works best in a loving environment where the child has received adequate positive attention.

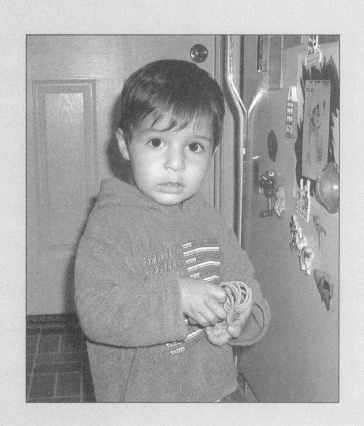

You say "YES" I say "NO"

You say "STOP" and I say "GO GO GO"

You say "GOODBYE" and I say "HELLO"

I don't know why you say

"GOODBYE" I say "HELLO".

Hello Goodbye
by Paul McCartney and John Lennon

Common Behavior Problems

DVD Chap 3&7

Temper Tantrums

Temper tantrums represent the stormy release of toddler frustrations. These are actually necessary expressions of your child's emotions before he can verbalize anger and frustration. They may occur frequently and more often when your child is tired, hungry or restrained for a long period of time (for example, in a car seat during a long trip.) You must teach your child that this is not an acceptable way of expressing his emotions. The earlier you address this behavior, the sooner it will begin to disappear.

What should I do during the tantrum?
The most important thing you can do when your child is having a tantrum is to remain unemotional and un-phased by this behavior — this is not easy! One suggestion is to pretend that you are an anthropologist on the Discovery Channel, watching a species of wild animal doing a ritual dance. Remove yourself emotionally from the scene. Remember — you are the parent in control, she is the child not in control.

Next, remove the audience. If you are alone at home, simply turn away and walk a short distance from your child. If others are around, remove your child to another room and remain close by.

It is very important not to abandon your child when she is having a tantrum. It is very frightening for your child to have a tantrum and she needs to know you will not let her totally lose control. If the tantrum goes on for longer than five minutes, place your arms around your child to help slow her down.

Give your toddler words for his feelings. Say gently, "I know you are angry" "I know you are upset." Over time he will begin to understand what these words mean. He will not have to act out his feelings as intensely if he knows you get the message.

When the tantrum begins to slow down, you can offer some soothing moments alone together. This lets your child know that you still love him and understand that he is upset.

What shouldn't I do?

Remember — if a tantrum is in progress — do not show your child that you are upset. Never hit your child during a tantrum. You do not want to reward your child, either positively or negatively, during a tantrum.

What if you are in a very public place such as a supermarket?

Experts are divided about how to handle this situation. One method is to leave the cart full of food behind and remove the child from the store to the car. He can have the tantrum alone. If it ends, you can finish your shopping. If not, remind yourself that this limit setting is more important at this moment than the groceries.

Another method is to allow the child to have the tantrum in the store. This can be very draining for you, the parent, however, for you may have to explain to the other customers and shop owners why you are blocking the aisle.

Breath Holding

Breath holding is an extreme form of temper tantrum in which the child can actually hold his breath until he is blue and may even pass out. Children cannot die from breath holding. However, they can hurt or injure themselves if they lose their balance and fall. If your child has had a breath holding episode, please call your pediatrician or family practitioner so they can rule out other causes for the loss of consciousness.

Recently a link between iron deficiency anemia and breath holding spells has been found and your doctor might want to check your toddler's blood for anemia or low iron levels. Some doctors may just try an iron supplement to see if it will help decrease the breath holding spells.

If they agree it is simple breath holding, you could try filling a spray bottle with water. As soon as your child begins to hold his breath, you quickly "spritz" the water in his face. This will usually stop the breath holding before it takes place.

Hitting

Aggression is normal at this age. Your toddler has no self-control, impulse control or any idea of what sharing means. This inevitably leads to expressions of aggression toward other children and even towards you. When this happens, you have to once again remain in control.

Do not hit your child, as this only teaches that it is okay for bigger people to hit smaller people.

Firmly take hold of your child and say, "No hitting!" and then remove your child quickly to another room away from the other children. Place him in time-out.

Do not speak to your child during this time. Afterwards, bring your child back to the group. If the behavior occurs again, do exactly the same thing. Remember, it is the consistency, not the severity of the discipline that works.

Hitting a Parent

Hitting a parent can cause a great deal of anxiety in your child and should never be allowed.

If your child hits you, immediately grab her firmly, say, "No hitting", and place your child in time-out. Do not look at or speak to your child for one or two minutes. With consistent responses from the parent, hitting can be stopped.

Biting

Toddlers bite out of frustration. Because a toddler's bite can break the skin and cause bleeding and bruising, it is one of the most unnerving expressions of their "toddlerhood." Human bites can also become infected and should be treated immediately with proper first aid techniques.

Your child will be socially rejected if she bites other children. Children are sometimes removed from day care centers or nursery schools if biting cannot be curbed. Parents are not immune from baby "jaws." If your toddler is biting, you will find yourself reacting angrily to the pain, which may interfere with your relationship.

Biting calls for strong methods. The first approach is similar to the approach for hitting. Take the child aside, look her in the face, and say, "No biting!" very firmly. Put her in the designated time-out area immediately.

If this approach does not work, you can introduce a negative taste association by placing a half-teaspoon of vinegar on your toddler's tongue before placing him in time-out. Do not do this in a punitive or cruel way. Your aim is to associate the bitter taste with the act of biting. For the association to be effective, this must be done as soon after the biting incident as possible. Although this may sound harsh, it is a very safe and highly effective method for reducing or eliminating biting behavior.

Do not bite your child back. He will not understand that you are trying to show him that it hurts when someone does it to him. It could backfire if your child sees this as an approach to anger modeled by you, the parent.

Head Banging

There are two types of head banging. One is another form of temper tantrum and should be handled in the same way. Rest assured — no matter how hard a child seems to bang her head, she never really hurts herself.

The second form of head banging is rhythmic banging of the head against the crib, and may occur before going to sleep or even as a form of self-relaxation in order to fall asleep. Although this is a harmless occurrence, it sounds awful. And no one knows why some children do this. Padding of the crib area with bumpers can help. However, discuss this with your family practitioner or pediatrician for more advice.

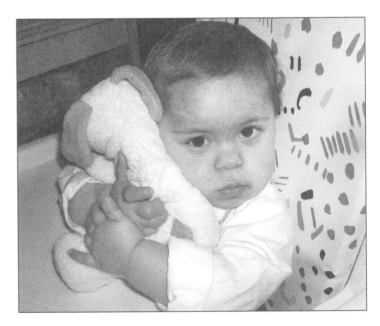

Fears and Phobias

Toddlers often develop irrational fears. These may even be fears of common household items, (such as a vacuum cleaner or the tub drain), dogs, bugs or imaginary monsters. Sudden fears are sometimes triggered by a frightening experience.

Psychologists feel that, in certain circumstances, these fears are a sign of an inner struggle taking place within your child. The monster may actually be your child's anger or other scary emotions, which are frightening for a child to have and difficult to express. Whatever the fear may be, to the child it is real and scary. You have to understand that and work with your child to overcome his fears.

You can start helping your child at home by playing some imaginary games with puppets or stuffed animals. Let your child write the script. Do whatever your child wants within the confines of the play. Don't try to challenge any situation or use this as an opportunity for teaching. Just observe where your child's subconscious wants to take you. Other good areas of expression are drawing or playing with clay or sand.

If your child suddenly develops a seemingly irrational fear or phobia, please bring it to your pediatrician's or family practitioner's attention so that he/she can discuss methods for handling this problem.

Too Much Routine
Providing routines for toddlers to help structure their world is part of good parenting. However, some toddlers may create their own routines and "rituals." They can become very demanding if their parents or childcare providers do not follow "their rules." For some this might mean only wanting to wear clothes of a certain color, or only eating food if each item on the plate is spaced apart. Some of this can be normal as a toddler tries to cope with life's frustrations. But if your child demands routines and rituals that are disruptive to your home or are very obsessive in nature, please consult your pediatrician or family practitioner. This can be a sign of stress in a toddler who is having a hard time adapting to the demands of his world.

"The family is both the fundamental unit of society as well as the root of culture. It represents a child's initial source of unconditional love and acceptance and provides lifelong connectedness with others.... Finally, a family is a perpetual source of encouragement, advocacy, assurance, and emotional refueling that empowers a child to venture with confidence into the greater world and to become all that he can be."

Marianne E. Neifert MD
pediatrician, professor and author.
Dr. Mom's Parenting Guide, ch.1 (1991).

Family Matters

What is a family?

A family is a person or persons and the child or children that they care for. A very simple definition that often gets lost in the political arena. Throughout time, children have been cared for by many different family members and in some cultures by a whole community. So if you are a single parent, or part of a non-traditional couple, or a grandmother or aunt caring for children, you are a family. If your child came to you naturally or through adoption, you are a family. Families are defined by love for and a responsibility to care for and safeguard babies and children.

Stress and Children

Anyone who tells you that they are never stressed by their children's needs or behavior is probably afraid to admit the truth. Along with all the good things children can bring into your life they also bring stress. It's a great responsibility and often parents are overwhelmed or just plain fatigued by everything that their children require of them. This is normal and it is why parents must have some time away from their children. Get a babysitter or ask a grandparent or another parent to help out. Go out and have some fun doing adult activities. Go to dinner, or a movie, or just plain hideaway for a weekend. It is necessary to recharge your physical and psychological batteries. Some parents feel guilty about leaving their children, and deny themselves these important breaks. This is a big mistake as the cumulative stress can take its toll.

If a parent is prone to depression or anxiety disorders, this prolonged stress can trigger symptoms, especially if accompanied by a lack of sleep. Any life-changing event that is occurring like a serious illness or death in the family, marital or financial difficulties, a move to a new home, or even pregnancy can cause a parent to feel overwhelmed. The symptoms of general depression include: overwhelming sadness, crying spells, loss of appetite, difficulty sleeping and an inability to feel happy with your children or with other aspects of life. Anxiety symptoms are more subtle but may include a sense of overwhelming uneasiness or panic attacks. When this happens, the person usually describes a feeling of impending doom, often accompanied by chest pain, shortness of breath, and/or rapid heart rate.

Many people do not seek help because they are ashamed or they feel that it will pass with time or more sleep. Some people hide their symptoms, but continue to feel miserable inside. This disorder is treatable, and it is important to treat. If you experience any of the symptoms listed above or you just don't feel *"right,"* let your physician know. (See the *Reference and Resources Section* for more information.)

Parent Time Out

Anyone who has ever been a parent knows that no matter how hard you try to control yourself, sometimes you lose it and <u>you</u> have the tantrum. Children know exactly how to push our buttons and sometimes you just have to scream. But hopefully you can pull yourself together, take a breath, put your toddler in a safe playpen or crib, and step outside on your front porch momentarily for some fresh air. Call your spouse or a friend, cry, laugh, put on some soothing music and just take a few minutes to calm down before retrieving your child. If you are having a really hard time, call a friend or neighbor to come over, and go for a walk. I'm sure you can repay the favor for them when they are having a "moment."

Parenting Multiples

Today many families are growing by two's and three's. And as you would expect, having two or three toddlers at the same time can be a very challenging experience. Get as much help as you can, and be sure to take some time out for yourself. Whether your multiples are identical or fraternal, the same sex, or different sexes,

you still have to consider individual temperaments and personalities as they become older. The same rules of limit setting apply whether you have one child or ten. In fact, when a household is filled with the joyous noise of childhood, it is even more important to maintain some sort of order. Safety issues are very important since you have to watch two or three very impulsive little people. So safe-proofing of the house should be a great priority. The safer the environment, the safer it will be when you cannot be everywhere at once.

Please consult the *Reference and Resources Section* for some books and web sites that can provide some more detailed information on raising multiple children. Also, many towns have support groups made up of mothers (and fathers) of multiples so that you will not feel all alone with your struggles and challenges.

Adoption

If your baby was adopted close to birth or as an older infant or toddler, it will have some effect on how attachment proceeds. A baby born in this country who is placed for adoption soon after birth will usually have a clear, well known pregnancy and neonatal history as well

as some family history. It is important to know about any drug or alcohol use during the mother's pregnancy because the effects will become more obvious in the second year of life when signs of fetal alcohol syndrome can be found.

If the baby was an international adoptee and had been in an orphanage setting without a close one-on-one caretaker, there may be physical problems such as growth catch-up and developmental delays as well as problems with attachment. So it is very important to consult a specialist in international adoptions to assess the health needs of your child and to help guide you on the special emotional needs of these children.

There is probably no need to raise the issue of adoption with a pre-verbal child. There will be opportunities during the preschool years when a child can form some type of understanding of the experience. For now, providing a stable, nurturing and loving environment and meeting the physical and emotional needs of your adopted child is most important.

Working Outside the Home

The decision of whether or not to return to work and when to return to work are personal ones and the decision should be made by you and your spouse or partner and determined by your own personal circumstances. Try not to be influenced by relatives, the media or the culture at large.

Children do well if they are cared for by people who care. It could be one-to-one care with a nanny or family member or a quality day care center. Don't be scared by the media stories. Most parents ultimately find a child care arrangement that works for their family and child. From time to time there are media reports of problems with children who attend day care centers, however, there have never been any large–scale, long-term studies that have shown consistent negative effects of childcare on children.

What is important with a toddler is making sure all childcare providers use consistent methods for discipline and limit setting, and that any environment that your child will be in will be safe and free of hazards.

More opportunities exist today for part-time or flexible arrangements for new parents. The childcare arrangement you ultimately select will depend on the baby, your finances and your work responsibilities. Only you can make this decision, but if you have concerns or questions, it is a good idea to discuss your decision with your pediatrician or family practitioner.

Working Inside the Home

All mothers work, whether they stay home or whether they work outside the home. There is too much conflict between these groups of mothers in some communities. If you feel that it would be best for your family, or for you, to stay at home and care for your children, then do it. The same advice applies. This is a personal family decision. Try not to be influenced by relatives, the media or the culture at large.

A New Baby

Having another baby while your child is still a young toddler can be like having twins. Double high chairs, double diapers, double strollers. And your toddler will have a curious reaction to this little "invader". Actually, toddlers between 15 and 20 months may have an easier time than an older child who has become more difficult in general and is in that stage when everything is "MINE" — including his parents.

Some experts recommend having another family member carry the infant into the house, leaving the mother free to reconnect with the younger child. An anxious toddler will want to have full attention from his mother even if he reacts with anger or disinterest at first. Buy a present and give it to your older child "from the baby" when you come home from the hospital.

Most children will have some feelings of jealousy towards the new baby and anger towards you. It's normal for the child to display these feelings and you can help by letting the child express his or her feelings without recrimination. It's important for the child to know that you still love them even if they have mixed

feelings. Of course in a pre-verbal developmental stage it will be difficult for your toddler to express these feelings with words.

But never leave small toddlers alone with a new baby. It is not uncommon for a toddler to hit or try to hurt the newborn unintentionally, of course.

Toddlers and Pets

Toddlers are toddlers and sometimes they can be overwhelming for a family pet. A child might unintentionally hurt a dog or cat by poking it, and the pet will understandably react with a bite or scratch. It's best to keep a close eye on both your child and the family pet when they are together and although it may take some time, teach your child not to provoke the animal in any way.

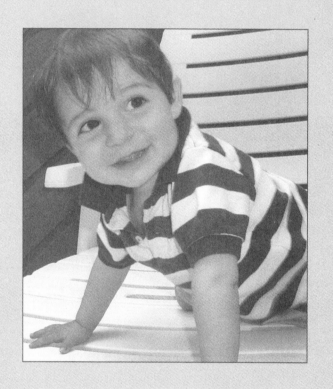

Syllabication: break·a·ble

Pronunciation: brk-bl

Adjective: Liable to break or be broken.

See synonyms at fragile. Noun: An article that

can be broken easily. We put the breakables

away before the toddlers arrived.

The American Heritage Dictionary of the
English Language. Fourth Edition, 2000.

Your Fifteen-Month-Old

Development

DVD Chap 1

The next few months are often described by parents as "trying"—because their small wonder is "trying" everything! Keep this in mind - They must explore and we must protect them. This may lead to daily conflicts and expressions of frustration. Your toddler now should be able to indicate his needs (without crying) through a combination of words and gestures.

Imitation is a form of learning, as your little one imitates you in daily work around the house. She will be studying your facial expressions and tone of voice. Your child will begin to pat or kiss pictures of animals.

In everything your child does, you will notice an improvement in fine motor skills. This includes attempts at self-feeding with utensils, drinking from a cup or building a tower of two cubes or blocks. If you are brave and provide your child with a crayon or marker, you will observe early scribbling attempts.

The ability to voluntarily pick up and release or hold objects is a major milestone for your toddler (who will practice this "casting" skill endlessly.) Although this appears simple, it is actually a complex skill. Your child

will not be able to build a tower of more than two blocks until this skill is mastered.

Another amazing development is the purposeful use of objects. Until now, your child was content to explore each object individually. Now you will see your child use a spoon to stir in a pan or use a broom to sweep the floor. He will use one object to reach another. This indicates that your child is starting to solve problems and use his imagination.

Your toddler will become interested in different shapes and sizes and will now attempt to fit shapes into other shapes. This may be frustrating at first. A shape sorter, puzzles and pots with lids work well in teaching your child this skill.

Another skill involves "nesting" or putting a series of smaller shapes into increasingly larger shapes. "Stacking" or putting smaller objects on top of larger objects is also an evolving skill.

Although your child may not be speaking in your primary language, he is definitely speaking! Jabbering strings of words will have definite meaning for your toddler, although it may seem a foreign language for you. This is called "tuneful jargon" as your child talks to you in an animated way, often acting out what she is trying to say.

Your child should be able to use at least three words other than Mama and Dada. He should be starting to name and recognize body parts and should be able to follow simple commands, "Give me the ball" and answer simple questions such as "Where is the dog?"

Along with improved language skills comes a finer appreciation of music and rhythm. Your performer will dance up and down or sway to music and delight in the repetition of favorite songs. In addition, your toddler will delight in filling the house with joyful noises.

As physical strength and coordination improve, so do gross motor skills. The range of normal ability at this age is wide and you may find your child beginning to walk one day and running and climbing the next. Most children will be able to creep up steps. Some may have figured out how to come back down (you can teach them how to "back down" the steps by having them imitate you or an older child.) Until this skill is mastered, please use gates on stair landings.

Feeding and Nutrition

As I have pointed out - your job as a parent is to offer your child healthy food in a nurturing atmosphere. It is his job to decide what and how much he will eat. You may need to tape record this message and play it under your pillow at night.

In practical terms, it means providing a balanced diet for your toddler, limiting sweets and salt. The nutritional needs of babies and toddlers are different from those of adults. Do not restrict fat and cholesterol, which are necessary for adequate growth. Do not give toddlers high fiber, low calorie foods, which may not have enough calories.

As you have already learned, you cannot make your child eat anything he does not want. In fact, the more you force, the more he will resist. Continue to offer a wide variety of foods, respecting his taste preferences within reason. If he refuses a meal, he will be hungrier for the next. Avoid the temptation to become a short-order cook as your child is likely to pass on the next selection as well!

Cow's Milk

Continue to give whole milk until your child reaches the second birthday with a maximum intake of 16 - 24 oz. per day.

Bottle vs. Cup

If you have not already done so, now is the time to begin weaning your child from the bottle. You can start by offering all juice and water in a cup during the day, then replacing the morning milk bottle with a cup of milk at breakfast. The last to go will probably be the evening milk bottle. This transition may be easy or difficult depending on the degree of attachment your child has for the bottle. Have patience and recognize the need for regression during periods of high stress, such as illness. To protect your toddler's new teeth, never have him go to sleep with the bottle or walk around with it in his mouth, especially if there is milk or juice in it.

Finger Foods

By now, your child should be self-feeding the majority of meals by hand. Encourage the use of utensils at this age. Buy a spoon with a wide, easy-to-grip handle. Sticky foods like cereal and mashed potatoes are the easiest for beginners.

Appetite

Most children experience a decline in their appetite at this age reflecting their slower growth rate. Your child may go through "food ruts" where he or she wants to eat the same food for every meal and refuses to eat anything else. Soon afterwards, however, most toddlers abandon the food of choice only to find a new favorite. Follow your child's lead within reason. Continue to offer a well-balanced selection of nutritious foods low in sugar, salt and additives.

Fear of New Foods

Most toddlers are slow to accept new foods. This is not surprising when you think of how many new things they encounter. Studies show it takes an average of ten offerings before a toddler will try a new food. When offering new foods, I suggest you just put it on the plate without pressure. Let your child decide when or if she will try it.

Snacks

It is easy to slip into bad eating habits with a young toddler. An occasional cookie, goldfish, pretzel or potato chip won't hurt your child, but a regular diet of these snacks can interfere with your efforts to provide a well-balanced diet. Try offering slices of fruit or cheese as snacks. Avoid candy. It promotes tooth decay and decreases your child's appetite for more nutritious foods. Excessive juice can cause similar problems.

Vitamins

If your child has no ongoing health problems or chronic conditions, and is eating a healthy well balanced diet, there may not be any need for vitamin supplementation. Discuss your toddler's need for vitamins with your doctor.

Fast Foods

You will be tempted by a variety of advertising and social pressures to visit fast food restaurants. Do this sparingly. Fast foods are generally very high in calories, fat and salt. For example, the salt content in a serving of French fries may be equal to all the salt you gave your baby during her first six months of life. Request nutrition information on fast foods. As an educated consumer, you can make better choices.

Choking Hazards

I highly recommend that you still avoid foods that pose a choking hazard such as nuts, hard candy, gum, popcorn, whole grapes, raw vegetables, uncut hot dogs and meat sticks.

Teeth

Teething

By 15 months of age your toddler will have several teeth. Remember there is great variability regarding the timing and even the pattern of tooth eruption. Much of this is determined by genetics. Don't worry if your baby seems to lag behind in the number of teeth, most children have the full set by 2 and 1/2 yrs of age.

Some children might have some mild discomfort during the eruption of a tooth. They may have excessive drooling and a strong desire to bite down on things (or people). You can help by using rubber teething rings or a frozen wet washcloth. Avoid using frozen teething rings because they may contain germs if the rubber is damaged and they usually are too hard on the baby's gums. If your baby is very uncomfortable, use acetaminophen or ibuprofen. But be careful not to overuse these pain medications.

Rarely a toddler might have a low grade (100 degree temperature) fever, or a period of loose stools during teething. But if your child has a temperature over 101 it is most likely NOT from teething. And if your baby's irritability seems excessive, you should call your doctor's office to discuss if your baby needs to be examined.

Tooth care

It's important to begin tooth care right away. In the morning and evening, begin cleaning the teeth with a soft toothbrush. It's best to use non-fluoride toothpaste at this age or just plain water.

Never put your baby to bed with a bottle filled with juice or milk. This can result in baby-bottle caries, a serious condition that can cause the loss of the baby teeth from decay.

Fluoride

Fluoride strengthens developing teeth and helps prevent cavities from forming. However, too much fluoride can cause a discoloration of the teeth called flourosis. If the water in your community is fluoridated, there is no need for any additional fluoride supplements. If the water is not fluoridated discuss with your doctor whether your toddler needs any supplementation. When given in the correct dosage fluoride is not a health hazard and will not discolor teeth.

If your baby does receive fluoride, be careful to avoid fluoridated bottled water or toothpaste that contains fluoride. Your baby might swallow the toothpaste while brushing.

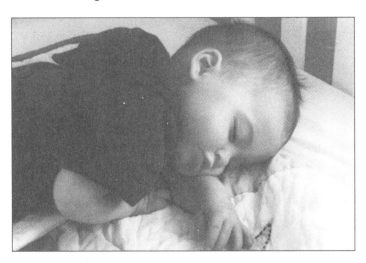

Sleeping

Naps
It is typical for a 15-month-old to take one nap a day, usually in the afternoon. Every child has a different sleep requirement, and some children won't nap at all, only to go to sleep at an earlier hour at night.

Nightmares
Along with your toddler's increasing imagination comes the ability to play out frightening visions in dreams. Your peaceful night may be pierced by the shrilling scream of your frantic child. It is difficult for your child to separate reality from fantasy. Don't let a scared child cry it out. Sometimes you may have to stay in your toddler's room to allow him to go back to sleep.

Toilet Training

Despite what friends or relatives may be telling you, IT IS TOO EARLY! (See the Chapter on *Toilet Training* for more information.)

Safety

The next six to eight months is the most dangerous stage of your child's life. Your house should be fully childproofed by now. Your active and mobile toddler requires a high degree of supervision. She should never be left unattended, except when sleeping in her crib. Never underestimate the abilities of your child. It's especially important to re-read the ***Blueprint for Safety*** found on page 37 with your active toddler in mind.

Safety Guidelines for Fifteen-Month-Olds

- The most important safety tip - **Never** leave a toddler unsupervised.

- Bathrooms and kitchens, in general, should be off limits unless supervised. These are the most dangerous rooms in the house.

- Be extra vigilant at other people's homes (especially if they do not have children.)

- Use safety latches, locks, and plug covers to childproof your home. (Buy safety kits that have everything that you need.)

- Make sure any childcare provider (even grandparents) follow these same guidelines.

Activities

DVD Chap 2

Games

As walking is achieved, your 15-month-old will delight in chasing and hiding games. Toddlers love to be chased by parents or older siblings. "I'm gonna get you!" usually brings squeals of laughter as the chase begins. They love to be caught, hugged and kissed.

Another game your toddler will love is to repeatedly bring objects to you or someone and then take that object back. We can't always see a method in his plan, but a simple "thank you" on your part will add to his good manners.

Nesting toys are great fun and you can watch your toddler be fascinated as he tries to figure out how to get smaller objects into larger spaces. Another great game is "fill the bucket" and empty it, over and over again.

No doubt, you will invent some games of your own.

Books and Reading

15-month-olds love to be read to. And reading is such an important activity to do with your child. And reading to your child is a great activity for all members of the family. Toddlers this age still want to hold and turn the pages of board books. Use books to name objects, animals and other things. This will help increase your child's vocabulary. Ask them to point to the "doggie" or the "truck". Simple stories are best for this age.

Music

Many tapes or records for children are available today. Even if your child cannot understand everything, the rhythms and music will delight him.

TV / Videos / DVDs

Excessive television watching is not healthy for toddlers. It is a passive activity and does not require much interaction on the part of your child. However, some limited viewing of age appropriate material is not harmful and can provide some good entertainment for your child and some welcome respite for you. There is no evidence that watching the same story repeatedly (over time) is harmful. It may be the equivalent of wanting a favorite story read over and over. It might reflect an issue that your toddler is struggling with.

Follow these guidelines for television viewing:

- Limit your toddler's television viewing (this includes videos and DVDs) to about one hour per day.

- Do not leave the television on in the background while your child plays.

- Select shows, tapes, or DVDs that include music, other children, animals and/or puppets. 15-month-olds are not developmentally able to follow a story line or plot.

- Avoid frightening shows such as action figure cartoons and the like. Even cartoon violence can be frightening to children of this age.

Toys

Always look for the recommended age for a toy. These recommendations refer to safety factors for the age, not the developmental level. Check for small or breakable parts or long cords, all of which present a danger to your child at this age.

The best toys for 15-month-olds:

- Nesting blocks and cylinders
- Stacking toys
- A shape-sorting box
- Colored plastic rings of different sizes that stack on a pole
- Pail and shovel
- Cardboard boxes, sturdy wagon or doll carriage
- A riding or rocking horse
- Pots and pans of all sizes
- Empty boxes
- Pull toys

Behavior

As I mentioned before, this can be a trying as well as a fun time for you and your child. Your 15-month-old will exhibit frustration and anger. You may see the beginning of temper tantrums, sometimes including hitting and screaming. Most behavioral pediatricians advise parents not to react emotionally when your child has a tantrum. Don't abandon her, but don't pay a lot of attention either. Without a reaction on your part, tantrums will

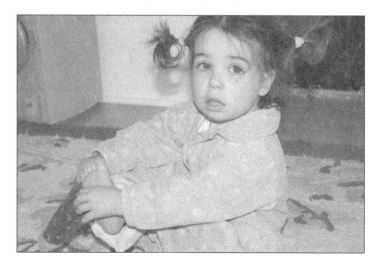

stop quickly. Remember—these are a normal part of your child's growing up.

Power struggles between children and their parents are very difficult to handle and much easier to prevent. The most common power struggle at this age involves feeding. Remember that there is a natural decline in appetite as well as a decline in caloric need as growth slows down. At this same time, your child is becoming more independent in feeding himself. My advice to you is to provide a variety of nutritious foods. Limit milk to 16 - 24 oz. per day, water down juices, limit junk food snacks and let your child's natural appetite take over. Don't panic about picky eating. One good meal a day is the norm for this age group.

The Next Doctor's Visit- Eighteen Months

You will probably return to your pediatrician or family practitioner when your child is 18 months old. If you have any questions or concerns before your child's next visit, do not hesitate to contact your doctor.

"I tell people that when my son was this age,

all of the things he did that really aggravated me

and got me upset were things that from the

standpoint of healthy child development,

I wanted him to do. I just didn't want him

to do them to me, or at those particular moments!"

Lawrence Kutner,
US psychologist and author.
Toddlers and Preschoolers, Ch. 5 (1994).

Your Eighteen-Month-Old

Development

DVD Chap 5

Socially, your young toddler will begin to imitate every thing that you do: carry a briefcase, sweep with a broom, vacuum with a toy or talk on the phone.

You will find your 18-month-old is very demanding of attention. He will test the effects he can have on the people around him and will begin to notice the various reactions different people have to him. Note - It's common for toddlers to remove their clothing (not always when you want them to!)

Your 18-month-old has greatly improved fine motor skills, which enables him to scribble spontaneously, usually in zigzags or circular lines. Use fat toddler crayons or washable markers and a large piece of paper and demonstrate to your child by making a mark and allowing him to imitate.

Your child should be able to build a tower of three to four cubes or blocks, will enjoy stacking and nesting toys, will be able to empty small objects from a jar by turning it over and will turn the knobs on everything. She will be able to turn one or two pages of a magazine or book at a time, too.

Your 18-month-old is beginning to appreciate shapes and will enjoy putting different shapes into a sorting box. He should be able to put a circle or square correctly in a form board (a board where the corresponding shape is cut out.) In addition, simple puzzles with small plastic holders in the center of the pieces will be enjoyable as your toddler learns to fit the pieces correctly.

The biggest milestone in motor skill development for this age group is climbing. It is also the most challenging milestone for parents. Once walking is achieved, your 18-month-old will be climbing everything like a mountain climber — he will climb the furniture "because it is there." This is a necessary skill for your toddler to develop. However, it also leads to more falls, bumps and bruises. So, it is also necessary for an adult to supervise all climbing efforts. This may lead to conflicts between the two of you, but with the right amount of supervision and limits, your toddler can enjoy safe exploration. Many areas now offer a play gym for children of this age to enjoy exploring and climbing in a padded environment. Check for one in your neighborhood.

Depending on when your child began walking, she may be walking quickly or even running by now. In addition, you will see her creeping backwards down stairs, scooping up toys from the floor without falling and making attempts at kicking a ball.

Your child will be able to point to body parts on request and may even name them. He may refer to himself by his own name, identify pictures in a book and say "bye-bye" when leaving. Over the next few months, some toddlers will begin to use two word phrases.

At this age, your 18-month-old will love to sing and listen to songs with repetitious phrases, such as "Old MacDonald's Farm." You may even hear him singing words and humming.

Language skills are also improving rapidly. Your toddler should be able to comprehend a great deal more than she can say. Most 18-month-olds have a vocabulary of four to ten words besides "Mama" and "Dada." She will also begin to name what she wants - "cookie," "juice." For some toddlers, their favorite word is "no!"

There is great variability in speech development, even among children of equal intelligence. It is not unusual to find an 18-month-old who says few words but understands everything. Comprehension is a good sign and usually means the words will follow by age two.

> **Warning signs there may be a problem with language development:**
>
> • If your child is not answering to his or her name
>
> • If your child is not pointing to objects
>
> • If your child is not making attempts to ask for what he or she wants
>
> Your pediatrician or family practitioner will follow your child's language development carefully over the next few months. If you have concerns, please discuss them with your doctor.

Feeding and Nutrition

Continue to provide your toddler three meals and one to two snacks per day, recognizing that his appetite reflects his slower growth rate. Offer a wide variety of healthy food and allow him to select what and how much food he will eat. Resist the temptation to give junk food if your 18-month-old does not eat a meal. He simply may not be hungry.

Milk
Continue to limit milk to 16-24 oz per day. See section on whole milk vs. low fat (p 14).

Juice
Juice should be limited to 4-6 oz. per day. Use water and add a small amount of juice for flavoring. Most toddlers will drink very watered down juice. Remember to continue avoiding carbonated beverages.

Bottle vs. Cup
If your 18-month-old has not transitioned from a bottle to a cup, it is time to do so. Never let your child take a bottle of milk or juice to bed.

What To Eat?

At this age, your child should be included in family meals. She should be able to eat most foods that adults can eat as long as they are cut into small pieces. Avoid power struggles over food. You can't win. Respect your child's food preferences within reason and restrict her access to excessive amounts of milk, juice and junk food. A hungry appetite will take care of the rest.

What Not To Eat?

Continue to avoid choking hazards such as nuts, hard candy, gum, popcorn, whole grapes, raw vegetables, uncut hot dogs and meat sticks.

How Much To Eat?

One good meal a day is average at this age. A good rule of thumb for toddler portion sizes is this - approximately one quarter of an adult portion size. The caloric requirements for an 18-month-old are minimal. So, don't worry! How they are growing is more important than how much they are eating! If you have concerns about your child's growth, discuss them with your pediatrician or family practitioner.

Utensils

You will notice a big improvement in the use of a fork and spoon at this age. Your proud self-feeder may be insulted if you try to assist!

Too Busy to Eat?

Your busy 18-month-old may have a limited attention span at mealtime. Understand that it can be difficult to stay seated when there is so much to do. I suggest you make it clear that when she gets down from the table, the meal is over. Do not offer more food until the next scheduled meal or snack. It will not take long before your toddler realizes where her bread gets buttered!

Vitamins

Most toddlers who eat a nutritionally balanced diet will not need vitamin supplements. Discuss with your doctor if there are special circumstances that might require additional supplementation with a multi-vitamin or iron.

Teeth

Teething
See p 79 (in 15 mo-old-section).

Tooth care
Continue to clean your child's teeth twice a day with a soft toothbrush. Use water or a non-fluoridated toothbrush if your child is receiving fluoride supplements or if the water in your community is fluoridated.

Lingering over a bottle of milk or juice can cause extensive damage to your child's teeth. The most severe damage occurs when your child is put to bed with a bottle. Dental work in this age group is difficult and frequently requires anesthesia. If damage is too extensive, teeth may have to be removed and permanent teeth will not come in for several years.

Fluoride
Discuss the need for fluoride supplementation with your pediatrician or family practitioner.

Sleeping

Cribs and Beds

The time to get a bed is when your child can climb out of his crib (and possibly injure himself.) This usually occurs around two-years-of-age, although it can occur earlier. A bed with a guardrail or a mattress on the floor can be used at this age.

Naps

One nap a day is still the norm for your 18-month-old.

Developmental Safety

Eighteen-month-olds run, jump, climb and get into everything. They can now try to open pill bottles or cleaning fluids. They will try to undo locks and safety latches. They will want to play with electrical outlets. And in general they will want to do whatever you *do* not want them to do. So keeping them safe is very challenging at this age. A certain amount of bumps and bruises is normal as they explore their environment. It's very common to see toddlers with large "goose eggs" on their foreheads or black eyes. But you can keep serious injuries to a minimum by following the **Blueprint for Safety** found on page 38.

Important Safety Notes

Here are some special highlights for this age:

- Concentrate on climbing related accidents.

- If they climb out of their crib, buy a bed now.

- Teach them to go down stairs backwards, but never let them do it unsupervised.

- Make sure cabinets with medicines or cleaning fluids are locked. Toddlers are known to put foul smelling and foul tasting liquids into their mouths.

- Look out for "nooses" such as window blind cords and cords on clothing.

- Supervise any activities near water.

Activities

DVD Chap 6

Games

Toddlers love to be chased by parents or older siblings. They love to run around in circles. Climbing on small age appropriate slides and climbing gyms is also great fun for them as they learn to enjoy their new large muscle skills.

Language games are great at this age. Asking your child to identify different animals and the sounds they make is a great language game. "What does the cow say?" "MOOOO!" Also naming of body parts and shapes and colors can be fun. Be careful, however, to keep these as games and not as instructions.

Play with blocks with your child and show them how to stack blocks in a tower. Laugh with them when they knock their blocks down. Roll a ball back and forth, or catch a soft or inflatable ball with your child. Avoid "real" sports. Your toddler needs to learn the basics first. Just holding a ball is a skill, he does not have to play baseball yet.

Books and Reading

Despite the fact that toddlers don't sit still for long, reading to your toddler is one of the best activities that you can do with your child. There is much evidence to suggest that the earlier you can begin reading to your child, the more they will love to read. In addition to parents, toddlers love to hear stories read by grandparents, aunts and uncles, and cousins. And make sure that any child care provider will also read to your toddler.

Eighteen-month-olds love picture books with simple stories about animals or small children like themselves. Board books can give way to paper pages as children this age love to turn the pages by themselves now. There is no harm in reading and re-reading favorite stories over and over again.

Music

Many tapes or CD's for your toddler are available today. Even if your child cannot understand everything, the rhythms and music will delight him.

There have been a lot of studies (and news reports) about the effects of television viewing on children – increased levels of obesity, violence, and most recently hyperactivity and attentional problems. The experts are still debating the findings but common sense tells us that prolonged hours of watching television - even with age appropriate content is never a good idea for any child, especially toddlers and preschool children. Leaving the television on in the background is also not healthy.

Follow these guidelines:

TV / Videos / DVDs

- Limit television or video viewing for your 18-month-old to no more than 60 minutes a day.

- Provide some toys for your child to play with while the television is on.

- When selecting any form of entertainment for your 18-month-old, look for those that include music, other children and/or puppets.

- Avoid videos that are "stories" because it is difficult for an 18-month-old to follow a plotline at this point.

- Avoid frightening shows such as "action figure" videos and the like. Even cartoon violence can be frightening to children of this age.

- Include videos that offer different more imaginative characters instead of the usual suspects, i.e. Disney, Barney, Sesame Street, etc.

Toys

Always look for the recommended age for a toy. These recommendations refer to safety factors for the age, not the developmental level. Check for small or breakable parts or long cords, all of which present a danger to your child at this age.

The best toys for 18-month-olds:

- Nesting blocks and cylinders
- Wooden or plastic blocks (that interlock)
- Shape-sorting box
- Pail and shovel
- Cardboard boxes
- Sturdy wagon or doll carriage
- Riding or rocking horse
- Pots and pans of all sizes
- Empty boxes
- Small riding car or tricycle
- Child size table and chair
- CD or tape player
- Set of puzzles with plastic knobs

Behavior

DVD Chap 7

The struggle for autonomy means becoming one's own person. For the 18-month-old, this means being separate from his mother and father. The infamous "terrible twos" actually start around 18 months of age. Parents have described the next twelve months as the most difficult period of early childhood. Depending on your child's temperament, this will be either easier or harder for you.

This stage of development peaks between 17 and 21 months for most toddlers and affects all aspects of behavior. It is critical that parents understand this normal developmental process.

Autonomy is a balance between independence and dependence. Your 18-month-old wants to be self-sufficient, but also needs to depend on you. In addition, your toddler's desires must be adapted to real world social and physical limitations. This may produce varying degrees of ambivalence or frustration in your child.

You will see this ambivalence clearly when your child is placed in a new environment. He will begin exploring by opening doors and entering new rooms. After exploring a little further than the "comfort zone," you will notice he will run back to you for an emotional "recharge" such as a hug or just a touch. Then, he will venture out again.

Other conflicts occur because your toddler's new developmental skills can get him into dangerous situations. Climbing is one example. Your child may become confused because he can't understand why his parents, who clapped and broke out the video camera when he started walking, are now yelling every time the new skill of climbing is practiced. It is important to provide safe play environments and to supervise climbing activities so that your toddler does not become inhibited. At the same time, you must set limits regarding potentially dangerous situations.

Your 18-month-old will now express her desire to "do it myself!" Even if she is not able to zip the zipper, she will refuse any help from you. She is strongly determined to do things her own way even if it may not be the best way. When safety is not an issue, it is wise to allow your toddler to use his own seemingly inefficient and primitive methods to show that you respect his determination and endeavors.

While two-year-olds are also famous for "negativism," this stage actually begins between 18 and 24 months. Negativism means saying "no" to almost everything that you ask. Even though your child may really want an ice cream cone, he will say "no" because he has to be opposite. While this drives parents crazy, it establishes your child's sense of power and control. Add to your toddler's lack of verbal communication skills, lack of patience, and the inability to make choices, and you begin to understand why this is such a difficult period for you and your child.

How to Cope with Negativism

Here again are some general principles and suggestions for coping with this developmental stage:

- Establish routines and rituals to help your toddler understand and have some control over his day. Routines are very important for your toddler at this age. He needs a certain order in his life and he depends on routines and rituals to accomplish this.

- Create an environment as frustration-free as possible. Safe-proof your rooms so she can explore.

- Use distraction and substitution. Be creative.

- As much as possible, avoid situations, which require long periods of good behavior and restraint. (Especially avoid fancy restaurants.)

- If your 18-month-old is tired or hungry, don't take him to the mall or force him to "enjoy" a long day at the amusement park.

**The Next
Doctor's Visit –
Two-Years-Old**

You will probably return to your pediatrician or family practitioner when your child is two-years-old. If you have any questions or concerns before your child's next visit, do not hesitate to contact your doctor's office.

The Toddler's Creed

If I want it, it's mine.

If I give it to you and change my mind, it's mine.

If I had it a little while ago, it's mine.

If it's mine, it will never belong to anybody else, no matter what.

If we are building something together, all the pieces are mine.

If it looks just like mine, it's mine.

—*Author Unknown*

Your Two-Year-Old

Development

DVD Chap 8

Your two-year-old can run, although he may have problems stopping and starting smoothly. He can jump in place and climb very well. He will be able to balance on one foot for a few seconds by two-and-a-half, but he will not be able to hop until age three. He can walk up and down a few stairs while holding on to the railing, but cannot alternate feet. Do not trust your child alone on stairs until this has been smoothly mastered.

Fine motor abilities have really improved. Your child should be able to turn the pages in a book one at a time. Right or left-handedness may not be fully developed until age three. Avoid attempts to change "handedness." Scribbling is becoming more involved and your child should be able to imitate (although perhaps crudely) a circle, straight line and "V" shape.

The Chatter Box is Born

Perhaps the greatest developmental achievement by two years of age is the ability to communicate with words. Your child should have a vocabulary of 60 words at minimum, but many children will have much larger vocabularies and will be able to name many common objects. She will be thrilled with the discovery that everything has a name (including herself) and she will enjoy naming everything as she goes along.

Most two-year-olds will begin to use two word sentences to express themselves. Don't worry about grammar! Appreciate your child's attempts at speaking in sentences. Show him that you understand what he is trying to say.

Imitative speech peaks during this period, with your child repeating everything you say. This is a good time to watch the words you choose! You can encourage your

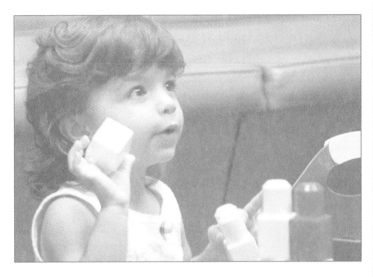

child's attempts at language by speaking clearly and avoiding "baby talk." Even though a mispronounced word may sound cute, avoid using the child's version, or it will stick.

As language expands, your two-year-old will enjoy nursery rhymes and stories even more than before. It is common for toddlers to make their parents read and re-read their favorite stories, often pointing out the animals and people. Favorite stories usually involve common childhood activities as well as animal stories of all kinds.

Routines

Your child at this age still has a poor concept of time (days of the week, minutes, hours) but will mark the day by the passage of routines. This is one reason why a regular routine is so important to a child of this age.

Feeding and Nutrition

Continue to provide a balanced diet for your child, limiting sweets and salt. Parenting a toddler means finding the right balance between setting limits and encouraging independence – and at this point, nothing may seem more difficult than feeding a two-year-old! Just remember, your responsibility as a parent is to offer healthy foods in a nurturing environment. It is your child's job to decide what and how much of what's offered he will eat. By fostering your child's independence at mealtimes, you are paving the way for healthy attitudes toward food. Your two-year-old is in a period of slow growth so his appetite may be small. Toddler portion sizes are generally one quarter of an adult portion size.

Milk and Juice
Limit milk to 16 - 24 oz. per day and undiluted juice to 4 - 6 oz. per day. You may begin using 2% milk, unless your pediatrician or family practitioner has advised you otherwise.

Battles Over Food

I hate to admit to this, but in battles over food, *you,* the parent, will almost certainly lose. The more you force your two-year-old to eat, the more she will resist. If this leaves you feeling out of control, take heart - you are really the one in control. You control the food you offer your child. Eventually, she will get hungry and eat.

If your toddler seems to be surviving on air alone, here are some suggestions:

- Review your child's growth with your pediatrician or family practitioner. If he is growing, he is getting what he needs.

- Generally, offer nutritious food that your child likes. If she ignores vegetables, just keep offering them. Some day she may decide to try them.

- Take the emphasis off food. Instead, praise your child for his use of utensils and good table manners. Allow her to take part in meal preparation. Two-year-olds love to help.

- Reduce your child's consumption of juice. Juice can lessen his appetite and cause "toddler's diarrhea."

- Resist the temptation to become a short order cook. This sets a bad precedent for the future. Provide one to two choices of foods that she has eaten well before. If she refuses a meal, be sure to offer a healthy snack at the next regularly scheduled eating time. If she doesn't eat, don't give anything but water until next snack or mealtime and make sure the snack is a healthy option.

- Do not beg, threaten or bribe. Mealtime should be pleasant for everyone.

- If your child is eager to get out of the highchair or booster seat, maybe it's time. Most two-year-olds do well in a junior chair.

Choking
Choking remains a concern until three to four years of age when children begin chewing with a grinding motion. So, again, avoid choking hazards such as nuts, hard candy, gum, popcorn, whole grapes, raw vegetables, uncut hot dogs and meat sticks.

Bottle
There is no physical reason for a two-year-old to drink from a bottle. If your child has a strong emotional attachment to the bottle, restrict the times it is used. You may wish to use it only for stressful moments or only at home. To protect the teeth, only allow water from the bottle. With other tasty beverages available, your two-year-old will soon find the bottle is no longer a desirable choice. Try using a sippy cup with a straw to help strengthen the muscles used in speech.

Vitamins

Most toddlers who eat a nutritionally balanced diet will not need vitamin supplements. Discuss with your doctor if there are special circumstances that might require additional supplementation with a multi-vitamin or iron.

Teeth

By 2 1/2 years of age most children have all of their primary teeth including their molars. By this time you should have identified a dentist, preferably a pediatric dentist or one who enjoys caring for children. A visit to the dentist at this age is recommended to make sure there are no abnormalities in the pattern of tooth eruption or in the gums or soft palate and that no tooth decay is developing.

Tooth Care

Continue to brush your child's teeth twice a day. You can begin using a fluoride containing toothpaste now but be sure to use only a "pea-size" amount of toothpaste on the brush. Encourage your child to spit out the toothpaste after brushing. If your child insists on brushing his own teeth, give him the brush without the toothpaste on until you can observe that he is actually brushing and not just sucking on the brush. Use a reward system for your child if she is refusing to allow you to brush her teeth. If all else fails, don't get stuck in a battle with a two year old. Wait till your child is asleep and run a washcloth over the teeth. It's not optimal, but it's better than nothing.

Fluoride

If your doctor has been prescribing fluoride drops as a supplement you might be able to change to the chewable tablets at this age. Ask at the two year old check up. Make sure you review if your child is getting the right combination of fluoride that balances protection against tooth decay and cavities against the risk of fluorosis – a condition of tooth discoloration from too much fluoride.

Sleeping

Toddlers are creatures of habit. They respond to daily routines, which provide order in their lives during a time of developmental confusion. That is why a bedtime routine is very important and will help your two-year-old make the transition to sleep.

Bedtime Rituals and Struggles – What to do

- Keep the bedtime routine short (no longer than half an hour) and simple. For example, after the bath.

- Read up to three stories, sing one song, say goodnight to the favorite stuffed animals, say goodnight, then it's lights out.

- You should make it clear to your child (who is no longer in a restrictive crib and can open doors) that you mean business. If he keeps coming out of the bedroom, he should be returned as many times as necessary.

- Use a reward system for staying in bed. You cannot force your child to go to sleep, but you can force her into a bedtime. What she does in bed after that time is up to her. This may take a lot of work in the beginning, but it will pay off later.

• The alternative to this method is staying with your child until he falls asleep. If your child becomes used to this, or if the child has been sleeping with you, the transition to sleeping alone may be more difficult. Most children should be able to go to sleep on their own by age three, even if they have been raised in the family bed.

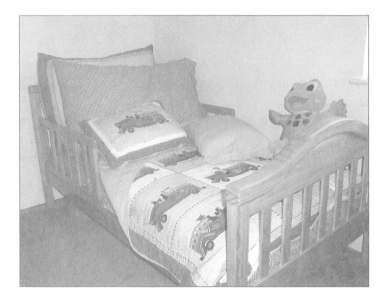

Bed vs. Crib
If you have not already done so, now is the time to get a bed with some type of bumper or guardrail. An alternative is to put a mattress on the floor; this is especially good for active sleepers.

Naps
Most two-year-olds still require one nap per day.

Toilet Training

It's time to assess toilet training readiness. Please review the Chapter on *Toilet Training* to see if your child might be ready to begin this training. Most toddlers will not be ready before two-and-a-half. The time not to start is at the height of "negativism." He will not want to do anything that you want him to do. Also if there has been a major change in your toddler's life such as a move to a new house or the arrival of a new baby, it's best to delay toilet training for a few more months to allow your toddler time to adjust to the new situation.

Safety

Developmental safety

Although children at this age are starting to get a bit more self-control, they are still impulsive. You may hear them telling themselves "NO!" as they try to hold themselves back from some dangerous activity. Keep in mind your toddler is not only curious, but also able.

> **Here are some safety highlights for this age:**
>
> • Keep your child in a car seat or booster, never just a lap belt.
>
> • Reinforce going down stairs backwards.
>
> • Even if they are taking swimming lessons, be six inches away from them at all times around water.
>
> • Cut food into non choke-able pieces. Avoid nuts.
>
> • Never let children put balloons in their mouths.
>
> • Make sure windows are locked or have window guards.
>
> • Cut the cords on window blinds and shades to avoid hanging.
>
> • Make sure guns have safety locks and are locked in a cabinet.

Games

When weather permits, take your two-year-old to the park. He will enjoy the sights and sounds, and the playground equipment. Climbing on small age appropriate slides and climbing gyms is great fun for him as he learns to enjoy his new large muscle skills. In the warm weather, small wading pools are great, as well as sand on beaches or sand boxes. A pail and shovel can occupy a toddler of this age for a long time.

Language games continue to delight your toddler. When you ask your child to identify different animals and the sounds they make, she will now act this out like a professional member of the theater. She will love to show off naming body parts. Sorting shapes and recognizing colors can be part of many games. You can even add numbers and letters. Be careful, however, to keep these as games and not as instructions.

Avoid "real" sports. Children need to learn the basics first. Just holding, throwing, or kicking a ball is a skill. He does not have to play professional sports at this age.

Books

Read! Read! Read! Your two-year-old will enjoy being read to and will begin to point out what will happen or start asking questions as you read. Picture books and age appropriate stories are important building blocks for a child's love of reading. She will often want to hear the same story repeatedly and will tell you if you skimmed over some parts. So even though it can be repetitive for you as the reader, it is an important part of your child's development.

Music

Two-year-olds love songs and music, especially songs with silly words and good rhythms. Look for music by Raffi ("Singable Songs for the Very Young"), Sharon, Louis & Bram ("Mainly Mother Goose"), Discovery Music Tapes, and Sesame Street and Barney.

TV / Videos / DVDs

This is a good time to start monitoring what your child is exposed to on television. Children have a hard time separating reality from fantasy and they think that what they see on TV is real.

Follow these guidelines:

- Avoid watching violent adult shows (or even older kid shows) while your child is in the room.

- Limit your child's television viewing to twice a day.

- Don't be alarmed if your child wants to watch one particular show over and over. Many experts feel this is no more harmful than re-reading a favorite story.

Toys

Always look for the recommended age for a toy. These recommendations refer to safety factors for the age, not the developmental level. Check for small or breakable parts or long cords, all of which present a danger to your child at this age.

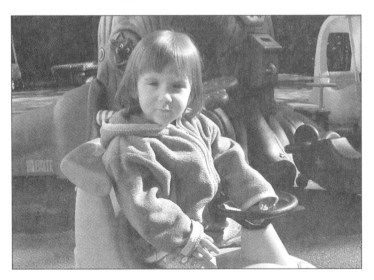

Best toys for your two-year-old:

- Wooden or plastic blocks (that interlock)
- Shape-sorting box
- Pail and shovel
- Cardboard boxes
- Sturdy wagon or doll carriage
- Rocking horse
- Tricycle or riding car
- Child size kitchen or workbench
- Child size table and chair
- Pots and pans of all sizes
- Toy fruit and vegetables
- Toy cash register
- Imaginary farmhouse or small doll house
- Set of small animals

- Puppets
- Dolls
- Toy trucks, cars, or trains
- Toy school bus
- CD or tape player
- Set of puzzles with plastic knobs

For the budding artist, crayons and markers, finger paints and lots of cheap paper! For the musician, toy xylophone, keyboard, toy piano, cymbals and rhythm toys. Earplugs for parents as necessary!

Behavior

DVD Chap 10

The "terrible twos" usually begins somewhere between 18 and 24 months and may last until 30 or 36 months of age. By now, you have most likely observed the two developmental stages, which make this the most difficult period of childhood:

1. The drive for Autonomy

2. Negativism

Autonomy

Through the struggle for autonomy, your toddler becomes an individual. It is probably one of the most important developmental tasks of early childhood. The first step for "parent survival" is to recognize the importance of the task, and to help and support your child through this time, despite the difficulties involved.

Autonomy is a balance between independence and dependence. Remember, your child wants to be self-sufficient, but he still needs to depend on you. This inner conflict leads to great frustration, which may culminate in crying or tantrums over seemingly unimportant things such as tying shoes or opening a zipper.

By two years, most toddlers can begin to learn self-help routines such as dressing and undressing, getting into a regular chair unassisted for meals, washing hands and brushing teeth. You must let your child try, even if he doesn't do things just right.

Developing autonomy also includes allowing your child to make some choices. It is best to limit them to a choice between two items. For example, in selecting clothing for the day, place two outfits on the bed and let your child choose one. Don't say, "pick something out of the closet," because too many choices will frustrate your two-year-old.

Allow your child to make decisions freely while playing, as long as safety is not an issue. Let him decide what the next activity will be. It is also important to respect your child's choice once it is made, even if it doesn't match yours. This helps build self-esteem and encourages creativity.

DVD Chap 7&10

Negativism

Negativism means saying "NO!" to everything that you ask (even if the answer is really "yes.") Your two-year-old is defining herself by contrasting with you. It is very frustrating for a parent because your child does not always mean "no" and does not think you will take him seriously when he really means "yes." After a while, you will begin to know the difference. (Remember how you learned to interpret your baby's different cries?)

To survive negativism, take a deep breath first! Remember that this is an important landmark for your child. This is an indication that your child has developed some form of internal organization. In other words, this is a sign of normal healthy development.

To cope with negativism, try to limit actual questions. For example, don't ask "Do you want to eat?" Say, "Time to eat."

Another way to cope is to make "no" a game. After asking a reasonable question like "Do you want some juice?" and hearing "no," ask some unreasonable questions like "Do you want an elephant?" with increasing silliness and "Do you want a spaceship?" (while you place a cup of juice on the table.) For those of you who love reverse psychology, say the opposite of what you really want. It may not work all the time, but it is worth a try.

Mine!

Another behavioral landmark is the comprehension of possession and ownership. Your two-year-old has learned the word "MINE!" Unfortunately, not everything really is and this may lead to conflicts with other children. Sharing is a foreign concept at this point, and should not be expected. Adult intervention is usually necessary to settle conflicts. You may talk about sharing, but it would be unfair to punish your child at this age for the inability to share.

Aggression

It is not inappropriate, however, to punish your child for aggressive acts, which may occur during this time including hitting, biting and hair pulling. Your child must learn that there are other ways to solve disputes besides acting out aggressive impulses.

Discipline

Your child's biggest fear at this age is the loss of parental approval. This is the cornerstone of all discipline at this age. He is learning internal controls but the process is not complete. You must help him by setting clear limits. He must learn the rules and discipline must be consistent among all childcare providers. Remember, it is the consistency, not the severity of the punishment that works!

Provide attention and affection throughout the day, and your child will not have to go to extremes to get it (and discipline will be more readily accepted.)

Physical and Psychological Discipline

Spanking or hitting as a regular form of discipline does not work. Any form of discipline, which is punitive, restrictive or coercive only teaches anger and rebellion and may cause an increase in undesirable behavior.

Avoid attacks on your child's self-esteem. Be careful not to attack your child's self-worth with statements such as "you're no good." Remember, it is the action you disapprove of, not the child!

If you find yourself yelling at your child or punishing your child constantly, if you are becoming enraged frequently by your child's behavior, or are using physical punishment out of anger, I suggest you talk to your pediatrician or family practitioner for help and advice.

The Next Doctor's Visit – Three-Years-Old

You will probably return to your pediatrician or family practitioner when your child is three-years-old. If you have any questions or concerns before your child's next visit, do not hesitate to contact your doctor's office.

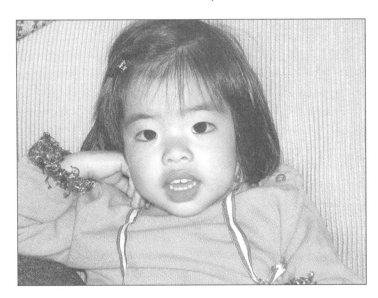

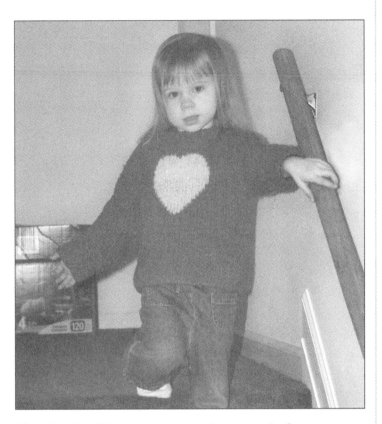

What's Next?   The *Preschool Years* are next and you are in for some real fun with your child. Noted child psychologist Selma H. Fraiberg referred to this time as "The Magic Years" and it is truly wonderful to watch your toddler turn into a three-, four- and five-year-old with his/her own ideas, lots of imagination and more verbal skills than most are ready for. It is a challenging time for you both as you try to balance your child's impulsiveness, natural curiosity and desire to explore his/her world with the need to become a civilized little person. There is much for them to master, both physically and emotionally. As a parent, you will be there to help them through each challenge. Just imagine – you will begin to see the world through their eyes and maybe, get in touch with that part of you that still remembers childhood. When that happens – and it will – it is truly magical.

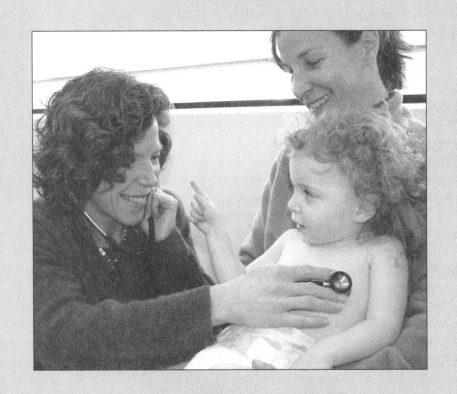

"The one who will profit most from the parents' relationship with the doctor is the child. Not only will he or she have better physical care because parents and pediatrician communicate well, but also he or she will sense the basic trust that exists in a good working relationship."

T. Berry Brazelton MD
Pediatrician and author
Doctor and Child 1976

Your Toddler's Pediatric Care

Scheduled Doctor Visits

The schedule of visits to your pediatrician or family practitioner may vary, but the following guidelines suggested by the American Academy of Pediatrics are most widely used:

Two Months to Two years

The American Academy of Pediatrics suggested schedule of well child visits is 2, 4, 6, 9, 12, 15, 18, and 24 months.

At each visit your family practitioner or pediatrician will look for expected developmental milestones. Feeding will be reviewed and safety issues, which pertain to babies at each particular age, will be reviewed.

A series of vaccinations will be given to your baby during the first two years of life. The schedule is frequently adjusted and may vary from state to state. Your pediatrician or family practitioner will guide you and provide you with a schedule. A test for tuberculosis is also given at some time during the first two years of life. In some states, a blood test to screen for anemia and lead exposure is also performed.

> **Recommended Vaccines:**
>
> DTaP – combined diphtheria, acellular pertussis and tetanus
>
> Hemophilus B (HiB) vaccine
>
> Hepatitis B
>
> Influenza vaccine
>
> IPV – polio vaccine
>
> MMR – measles, mumps and rubella
>
> Pneumococcal vaccine
>
> Varivax – Chicken pox vaccine

Immunizations

Why do we immunize?
We immunize our children to protect them from very serious and often life-threatening diseases. Vaccines provide immunity by introducing the disease in a weakened or killed form into the body. The body's immune system then produces antibodies to the disease and this provides immunity. The only other way to gain immunity is to actually have the disease.

Are there risks to my baby from vaccines?
Overall, the risk to your baby's health from these vaccines is very small. The most frequent side effects are fevers or rashes, or swelling at the site of the injection. Some vaccines, however, carry more risk then others for serious side effects. Your pediatrician or family practitioner will discuss these risks as well as the benefits of the vaccines before your child receives them. You will also receive written information about the vaccines. Please read this information carefully and ask any questions before your child receives the vaccines. It is the overwhelming conclusion of both the American Academy of Pediatrics as well as the Centers for Disease

Control (CDC) that the benefits to immunization outweigh the very small risks involved. However, you must feel comfortable making this decision.

Is there a relationship between the MMR (Measles, Mumps, and Rubella) vaccine and ASD (Autistic Spectrum Disorders?)
In recent years, this question has been raised in many public forums. Scientists generally agree that most cases of ASD result from events that occur before a baby is born or shortly after birth. However, the symptoms typically emerge in the second year of life—about the same time the MMR is administered. Because of this, there has been concern that there is a relationship between the MMR vaccine and ASD.

In response to these concerns, the Centers for Disease Control and Prevention (CDC) and the National Institutes of Health (NIH) asked the Institute of Medicine (IOM) to establish an independent expert committee to review all hypotheses regarding this question. (The full report can be read on www.CDC.gov/NIP also see www.AAP.org.)

The committee concluded that the vast majority of cases of autism cannot be caused by MMR vaccine and that the recent increasing trends in autistic diagnoses cannot be explained by the rate of immunization with MMR in this country. Research and review continues into the safety of all vaccines and the establishment of an independent scientific committee of this purpose is an important step forward in vaccine safety.

Is thimerosal used as a preservative?
Thimerosal is a preservative that was originally used in some vaccines to stop the growth of bacteria. There is no evidence that thimerosal containing vaccines cause any harm in children, and no link has been found between thimerosal and ASD (Autistic Spectrum Disorders). Yet some researchers raised concerns about exposing small infants to mercury in the thimerosal. Therefore the FDA and the pharmaceutical companies decided to remove

thimerosal as a preservative from all routine childhood vaccines. It still exists in some preparations of the influenza vaccine, however, it is not thought to pose any risk for the infant receiving the vaccine. Since influenza vaccine is now recommended, the supplies of preservative free vaccine will probably be increased over the next few years.

Do I have a choice?
All parents have a choice. You should be provided with information on the risks and benefits of each vaccine so you can make an educated decision. It is the recommendation of the American Academy of Pediatrics that all children be as fully immunized as possible in order to protect our children and society from these contagious and dangerous diseases.

Is immunization required for school entrance?
Every state has its own requirements for vaccination. Some states are very strict about vaccinations and school attendance. This is especially true for pertussis and measles vaccines, and some children have been barred from school or day care until the vaccine was given.

If you decide not to immunize your child at all or only to immunize with certain vaccines, it will be your responsibility to deal with the local school board. Your pediatrician or family practitioner may or may not get involved unless there has been a medical contraindication to receiving the vaccine.

Does my child have to get the shots at the doctor's office?
Most pediatrician or family practitioner provide the vaccine as a service to their patients. You may be able to obtain these vaccines at your town's local health department or clinic. At most clinics, the vaccine is administered free of charge for eligible patients. If your child does not receive his vaccinations at your family physician's office, please let them know the date of the vaccination, so that they can keep your child's records up-to-date.

What are the diseases vaccines immunize against?

Diphtheria is a severe infection of the nasal and breathing passages. A toxin is released into the body and can cause other areas (such as the heart and neurologic system) to become affected. Ten percent of infected patients die from this illness. Vaccination against diphtheria has been so successful in this country that there are fewer than five cases each year in the United States.

Tetanus (also known as lockjaw) can result from contaminated wounds or punctures. A toxin is released into the blood, which causes stiff neck and difficulty swallowing, followed, by painful muscle spasms. It is almost always fatal.

Pertussis (also known as whooping cough) begins with a mild cough and cold but then progresses to severe paroxysms of coughing ("the whoop") often followed by vomiting. Breathing becomes difficult because of the coughing spasms.

Even after the whooping stage, the patient can be ill for many weeks with cough. Other complications include convulsions, pneumonia, and neurologic damage or death. The disease is very severe if it occurs during the first year of life. For infants less than eight months, the death rate is one percent (1%) of infected children. There are still 3,000 to 4,000 cases reported in the United States each year, and many more mild cases occur in adults each year. There is no cure for pertussis and care is usually supportive in the hospital.

Polio results from a virus. Most cases occur without any symptoms or present as a very mild flu-like illness. Permanent paralysis can result.

Measles is a viral illness. Patients have a cough, cold symptoms, red eyes and a distinctive red rash that looks as if a bucket of red dots was poured over them.

Most cases are uncomplicated but pneumonia is a common complication. Less common is encephalitis (or inflammation of the brain) in one out of 2,000 cases. Survivors often have permanent brain damage. Death occurs in one out of 3,000 cases in the United States.

Mumps is a viral disease that causes swelling of the salivary glands. Encephalitis is a complication of mumps. Orchitis (infection of the testicles) occurs in post-pubescent adolescents and adults. This can lead to sterility.

Rubella is also known as **German Measles.** This viral infection produces very little illness in healthy children and adults. It involves a rash, some lymph node swelling and fever.

We immunize children to protect infants from congenital rubella. This occurs when a woman who is pregnant gets rubella. The disease is devastating to her unborn child: deafness, eye abnormalities, heart defects and neurologic problems including mental retardation can result.

Hemophilus Influenza (HIB) is caused by a bacterium, not by a viral flu. It is a very common cause of infection in infants and children. The most serious infections caused by this bacterium are epiglottitis (swelling of the epiglottis or upper airway, which can rapidly become fatal) and meningitis. Although meningitis can be treated with antibiotics, complications such as deafness, brain damage, and death can still occur.

Chicken Pox (Varicella.) The majority of cases of chicken pox are uncomplicated. The child is uncomfortable for a week with itching, and sometimes pain and fever. Some cases develop complications, a few of which can be life-threatening. Before the vaccine was used, every year, between 50 and 100 people died from complications of chicken pox, half of whom were children. The most common complications in otherwise healthy children are skin infections—some of which can be very severe and even produce toxic shock syndrome—and pneumonia. Adolescents and adults can get the most severe cases of chicken pox with a higher complication rate. Less serious complications such as the potential scarring of chicken pox lesions are also a concern to many parents.

The varicella vaccine - Varivax - is a protection against chicken pox, but it does have some drawbacks. Natural chicken pox gives a person life-long and complete immunity from the disease. The vaccine does not guarantee 100% immunity. In clinical trials, the vaccine was effective 70–90% of the time. If a child who has had the vaccine does get chicken pox, however, it will be a milder form of the disease.

Protection from the vaccine may not last forever. Protection is known to last for 20 years, and researchers continue to follow and study this issue to determine if a booster will be needed.

Pneumococcus. Pneumococcal bacteria causes many infections in infants and children. The most serious of these infections are pneumonia and meningitis. Pneumococcus is the leading cause of bacterial meningitis in the United States at this time.

Hepatitis B was added to the list of diseases children should be immunized against by the American Academy of Pediatrics in 1992. Hepatitis B is a virus, that attacks the liver. Even though most illnesses are over within a few weeks, a percentage of patients go on to develop a chronic form of the illness, and this puts them at greater risk to develop liver cancer.

Hepatitis B can be acquired through exposure to blood or blood products, from sexual contact, and from mothers to infants at the time of birth. Most mothers are screened today while they are pregnant so that the doctor knows which mothers are carriers of the disease, and which infants need special treatment at birth. In rare cases, Hepatitis B can be acquired through close contact within families, from person to person through contact between open skin lesions, and possibly through saliva to mucous membranes (inside the mouth.)

Even though the highest risk period for infection is during adolescence and young adulthood, immunization of all infants is the goal. The advantages to immunizing infants are that they are immunized while they are within the healthcare system, and the dosage required (and therefore the related costs) are less. If an infant should contract Hepatitis B, he or she is more likely to develop the chronic form of the illness, so early vaccination is advantageous. The disadvantage is that researchers are not certain how long the vaccine protection will last, and there is a chance that your child may need a booster during adolescence or young adulthood.

Influenza. Although we commonly refer to a variety of viruses as the flu, the "true flu" is caused by the influenza viruses. These are very contagious and can spread rapidly through families, schools and offices. The symptoms are very specific and for older children and adults include high fever (usually lasting 4 - 6 days), sore aching muscles, generalized weakness, and headache, pain behind the eyeballs, a sore throat and hacking cough. More serious complications include pneumonia, encephalitis (inflammation of brain tissue) and serious secondary infections with bacteria. It is the overwhelming bacterial infections and respiratory complications that can be most deadly for young infants and are responsible for most of the hospitalizations. Although the majority of patients, including most infants and children, will recover fully, some patients will become seriously ill and require hospitalization.

Influenza can be a deadly disease for young infants and because of an increase in the deaths of healthy infants and children from influenza, the American Academy of Pediatrics is now recommending routine annual vaccination of all infants 6 months of age to 24 months of age. This will require two shots if the infant is receiving this immunization for the first time. It is also recommended that household contacts of children under 2 years of age also be vaccinated.

When to Call Your Doctor's Emergency Line: You are the best judge of your baby's health. If, at any time, your child does not "seem right" to you, call your pediatrician or family practitioner. Learn to trust your instincts. Apart from that, you should call your doctor's emergency line if:

- A baby under three months of age has a temperature of 100.5° F or greater (taken rectally) or an older child has a rectal temperature greater than 105° F.

- "Projectile" vomiting (vomiting which seems to go across the room) occurs or repeated forceful vomiting especially if the vomitus contains blood or green bile.

- If your baby is bleeding heavily from a cut or wound.

- If your baby's stools contain more than a small amount of blood.

- If your baby is acting very irritable and lethargic or inconsolable (with decreased or no periods of alertness, no sucking or no eye contact.)

- Listlessness is present—the baby does not seem to interact with anyone while awake.

- Your baby is breathing very rapidly, you hear wheezing noises or continuous coughing is present.

- Croup (a barking sound made when your child coughs) especially in a small infant or if croup symptoms are unresponsive to steam or cool air.

- Stridor (a harsh noise made by an infant or child on inspiration.)

When to call
911 or the
Rescue Squad

There are some problems when it is best to call 911 before calling your pediatrician or family practitioner's office. Make sure the phone number is posted near every phone in the house.

- Severe difficulty breathing, especially with blue coloring or after choking.

- Serious injury (especially with massive bleeding, obvious broken bones or severe head trauma with loss of consciousness.)

- Electrical shock or burn.

- Allergic reaction (especially with difficulty breathing, airway swelling or wheezing or any of the above with hives.)

- Near drowning.

- Unconsciousness or an infant or child that cannot be easily awakened.

When to call
Poison Control

Call any time an infant ingests a potentially poisonous substance or plant. If severe breathing difficulties or any of the above severe reactions are present, however, call 911 first.

REMEMBER TO CALL **POISON CONTROL** FIRST BEFORE CALLING YOUR PEDIATRICIAN OR FAMILY PRACTITIONER'S OFFICE AFTER AN INGESTION. Post your local poison control number near every phone in your house.

Note: The Academy of Pediatrics no longer recommends the use of syrup of ipecac after an ingestion or poisoning. Discard any bottles you may still have at home.

Common Symptoms and Illnesses

This section is not meant to be an all inclusive listing of medical problems that occur in infancy. These are just some common problems and what you need to know. Whenever you need help with a sick infant, your pediatrician, family practitioner and their office staff will be there to help guide you.

Giving Medication

Typically, medication is given as either 1/4, 1/2 or one teaspoonful. Instead of estimating these measurements with an ordinary kitchen spoon, ask your pharmacist for a special medicine spoon or syringe.

Some infant medications (such as Tylenol, Advil and Motrin) come with their own droppers. These droppers should be used only with their respective medications.

Some medications should not be given with food or drink because this will interfere with absorption. You may find that if you have to force your young one to take the medicine he may gag. If this is the case, it is better to give the drug on an empty stomach.

Other medications should be given with food. If special instructions are needed, you will receive these with your child's prescription.

Important Medicine Notes:

• Since the concentration of medicines is not equal in drops and elixirs, never use one dosage with the other.

• An ordinary teaspoon does not equal a dropper.

Colds

Should your toddler develop a simple runny or congested nose without fever, you can begin treatment with salt water nose drops (1/2 tsp. salt added to eight ounces of warm water) or salt water nasal spray (Nasal, Ocean.) Place two to three drops or one spray in each nostril. If the mucous is visible at the tip of the nostril, and your toddler will allow it, use a bulb syringe to remove the mucous. Bulb syringes are also known as nasal aspirators and may be labeled "ear syringe." Don't overdo the use of the bulb syringe, however, since it can irritate the child's nose. A cold water vaporizer will help to keep the room moist and the secretions loose.

Now that your baby is older, you can use Over the Counter (OTC) cold medicines. All have a decongestant and usually an antihistamine. They can help relieve symptoms and make your baby more comfortable. However, they do have some side effects. Decongestants can make your toddler irritable and cause difficulty sleeping. Antihistamines dry secretions and make it more difficult for your child to get rid of them. Follow directions from your doctor's office and never use more than the recommended dosage.

Antibiotics serve no purpose in the treatment of the common cold and should not be expected. Remember, the cold symptoms usually bother the family much more than they do your toddler.

Constipation

If no stool is passed for more than four days, if the stools are hard and ball-shaped, or if your child appears to be in pain when passing the stool, this may represent constipation. Simple remedies include giving your child some prune juice to naturally help things along. Your doctor may recommend a glycerin suppository or prescribe some mineral oil to help lubricate the stool. Before beginning any treatment, discuss the options with your pediatrician or family practitioner.

And if there is blood on the diaper or in the stool, please notify your doctor so he/she can make sure it is simply local bleeding from passing a hard, formed stool.

Avoid the regular use of suppositories, baby enemas, rectal stimulation, or home remedies.

If constipation is accompanied by vomiting or a distended abdomen, call your pediatrician or family practitioner immediately.

Diarrhea

Diarrhea stools are watery and may be foul smelling. An increase in frequency and amount of stool may be noted.

Current recommendations are to allow your toddler to feed through uncomplicated diarrhea. This means that if the child is not vomiting and is not showing signs of dehydration, you can continue your toddler's regular diet. If you are breastfeeding, continue nursing throughout the bout of diarrhea.

You may want to supplement with oral re-hydration solutions (such as Pedialyte or Infalyte) if you cannot keep up with the stool losses. Your doctor will advise you if this is necessary.

If cow's milk which contains lactose seems to make the diarrhea worse, you can temporarily start feeding your toddler soy milk or a lactose-free milk product. Let your child drink as much as he wants as often as he wants. You can maintain your child on this milk for at least one week before going back to regular cow's milk.

You can continue solid foods (if your child is not vomiting) but try mild binding foods first such as bananas, applesauce or Jell-O. Avoid other fruits and vegetables. Rice is usually a good choice as well. For older infants, salty crackers can be given. The well known BRAT (no reflection on the child's behavior) diet consists of Bananas, Rice, Applesauce and Toast. These foods have been shown to help bind a child with diarrhea and the acronym makes it easy to remember.

Dehydration   When stool losses are not replaced by oral fluid intake, dehydration results. The signs of dehydration include a dry, sticky mouth, absence of tears, decreased urine output (no urine in a 6-8 hour period) and a poor appearance overall. If this occurs, notify your pediatrician or family practitioner immediately.

Diaper Rash   If a rash is developing, change your child's diaper frequently and immediately after soiling. Avoid occlusive diaper covers, especially at night (you can make the diaper "breathe" more easily by snipping the elastic leg bands around rubber pants or by cutting slits in the plastic covering of disposable diapers.) Apply barrier cream liberally with each diaper change. These protect the skin by sealing out humidity and irritating factors that may be present in urine or stool. These also reduce friction.

You don't have to remove all of the previously applied ointment with each diaper change. Superficial cleansing followed by another application of ointment is sufficient. If diaper rash persists more than a few days, a yeast infection may have developed. Try adding an anti-fungal ointment such as the brand Lotrimen (sold over the counter as athlete's foot cream) with each diaper change.

Ear Pain

Although it may be difficult to tell in a toddler if they are experiencing ear pain, there are some clues. If your child cries whenever placed down to sleep or laid down flat on a changing table, or if he bats at his ear with a hand, or if he seems unusually fussy, this may indicate the presence of an inner ear infection. This is especially true if your toddler has signs of a cold or has a fever. If you suspect your child may have an ear infection, call your pediatrician or family practitioner to have him/her seen.

Fever

Fever is your child's normal response to infection and is often the very first sign that an illness is starting. It is also a common cause of anxiety in parents and a frequent reason for calling the doctor's office.

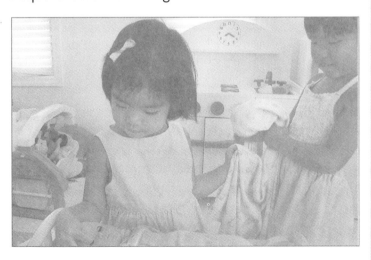

Taking the Temperature

Purchase a digital thermometer, which is easier to read. Avoid the use of temperature strips on the forehead, as these are inaccurate. Also avoid an ear thermometer in infants and toddlers, which do not work well with small ear canals. Once a child is older, they can be useful to identify fever, even though they are not always as accurate as a rectal thermometer.

Axillary temperatures (under the armpit) can be quite accurate if the toddler can sit still long enough to hold the thermometer under the arm. Likewise, a rectal temperature can be taken if the toddler can cooperate and hold still for about a minute.

To take a rectal temperature, first lubricate the tip then place into the rectum (about 1/4 to 1/2 in deep). Pinch the cheeks of the buttocks together to hold the thermometer in place. Wait two minutes or until the digital thermometer beeps. Remove the thermometer and read it. Any temperature over 100.5° F is considered a fever. Body temperature varies during a 24-hour period and is usually higherat night than in the morning.

Toddlers typically have temperatures between 102° F-104° F. Fever can accompany a simple viral infection or indicate a bacterial infection such as in the inner ear, bladder, throat, or chest. In rare cases it can mean that the child has a blood infection or brain infection such as meningitis. It's important to remember that fever in and of itself is not dangerous. It is true that children between six months and six years can experience a convulsion with fever, but this only occurs in five percent of children. As frightening as the convulsion is, it is usually very short and causes no long-term damage to a child's brain. Of course, if this occurs you should call the rescue squad or take your child to be seen immediately to rule out any other problems.

The height of the fever is not as important as how your child looks, especially after an initial treatment with acetaminophen or ibuprofen. No one looks great with a high fever, but a half hour after the medicine or a lukewarm bath, the child should look a bit brighter. If your toddler can nurse or drink some liquids, make eye contact, or maybe even smile at a familiar face, it's more likely to be a simple infection. But if your child is very lethargic, avoids eye contact, has no moments of playfulness or interest in other people or toys, then the illness may be something more serious.

When should you call your pediatrician or family practitioner about a fever?

- If your child has a fever and is very lethargic and does not improve after getting acetaminophen or ibuprofen.

- If your child does not make eye contact, respond verbally or smile.

- If your child is having difficulty breathing.

- If a fever is accompanied by a rash, severe sore throat, deep coughing or wheezing, a stiff neck, headache, severe abdominal pain, severe vomiting or pain on urination.

- If your older infant or toddler has a temperature greater than 105° F. Remember, too, if you also have an infant (a baby less than three months) who has a temperature greater than 100.5° F, you should call your pediatrician or family practitioner.

- If fever lasts more than three days.

Fever Treatment

We treat fevers in small children to make them more comfortable. If your child has a temperature of 101° F and is running around playing, you may not need to do anything at all. The treatment for fever is using a medication such as acetaminophen (Tylenol) or ibuprofen (Advil or Motrin) and following the directions for your child's weight and age. Be careful not to use a teaspoon when a dropper is indicated. The older child syrups and suspensions are not as concentrated as infant drops.

Another method is to give your child a lukewarm (not ice cold) bath. You don't have to immerse the child in water, rather lightly rub water over the child's body to help evaporate the heat. It is best to do this 30 minutes after giving acetaminophen or ibuprofen to avoid chilling.

Drinking lots of cold liquids will also help bring down the body temperature. Increasing the amount of fluids is also necessary in children with fever because they can become dehydrated more quickly.

Remember to avoid alcohol baths or rubs (children can have convulsions from alcohol toxicity absorbed through the skin). Dress your child in light cotton underwear and pajamas to prevent the temperature from rising higher. Avoid layering of clothes or blankets, high room temperatures, or hot outside temperatures. Avoid aspirin or any product that contains salicylates (Pepto-Bismol) to avoid Reyes' Syndrome, a potentially deadly illness.

Fevers that accompany uncomplicated viral illnesses such as colds and sore throats usually last three to four days. If your child has a fever that lasts longer than three days it is wise to call your pediatrician or family practitioner and have your child evaluated.

"Pink Eye" or Conjunctivitis

If pus develops in the eyes, it will appear moist and gooey. This may mean that a common eye infection (conjunctivitis) is present. This can be treated with an antibiotic ointment. Call your pediatrician or family practitioner and he/she will prescribe the medicine. This infection does not cause impairment of vision and is not dangerous.

Vomiting

Some toddlers will spit up once or twice if something upsets their stomach, but a true stomach virus will declare itself by repeated vomiting, often several times in an hour. The typical stomach virus lasts less than 24 hours. The worse and most frequent vomiting occurs in the first 6-8 hours. After that, the time between vomiting will begin to slow down. If no diarrhea is present, it is unlikely that a healthy toddler will dehydrate in a twelve hour period. So there is no need to force a vomiting child to take fluids. They will most likely be vomited right up. After the vomiting has slowed down you can begin to give small amounts of an oral rehydration solution such as Pedialyte. Give small sips (less than an ounce at a time) frequently rather than a large amount of liquid that will surely be vomited right back. If vomiting lasts greater than 24 hours and if it does not seem to slow down after the first twelve hours, please notify your pediatrician or family practitioner.

BOOKS

**General
Information**

Caring For Your Baby and Young Child: Birth to Age 5, by Steven P.
Shelov, M.D., F.A.A.P. The American Academy of Pediatrics, Bantam
Double Day Dell Publishing, 1998
A great reference book. Covers a wide area of questions.

What to Expect the Toddler Years, by Arlene Eisenberg. Workman
Publishing, 1996
A continuation of the series.

Touchpoints: Your Child's Emotional and Behavioral Development
by T. Berry Brazelton. Perseus Press, 1994
Great book on the stages of development and a caring approach
to children of all ages.

*The Girlfriends Guide to Toddlers: A Survival Manual to the "Terrible
Twos"* by Vicki Iovine. Perigee, 1999
A continuation of the series.

1, 2, 3 The Toddler Years: A Practical Guide for Parents and Caregivers
by Irene Van de Zande. Santa Cruz Toddler Care Center, 1993
Wonderful book. So well written and covers the emotional
word of a toddler very well. Gives excellent advice.
I recommend strongly.

Games to Play with Toddlers by Jackie Silberg. Gryphon House, 1993
What to do when there's nothing to do.

*Parenting Your Toddler — The Experts Guide to the Tough and Tender
Years* by Patricia Henderson Shimm. Perseus Books, 1995
Written by the Director of the Barnard College Center
for Toddler Development. If you want to really understand your
toddler's world, read this book. Great suggestions for handling
most problems.

Temperament

Temperament Tools — Working with Your Child's Inborn Traits by Helen
Neville and Diane Clark. Johnson Parenting Press, Inc. 1998

Raising Your Spirited Child by Mary Sheedy Kurcinka. Harper
Perennial, 1991
Written for parents who are having difficulties with their children.

Nutrition

Guide to Your Child's Nutrition by William Dietz M.D. and Lorraine Stern M.D. The American Academy of Pediatrics, 1999
Gives you all the facts and covers it all from infancy to adolescence.

Dr. Paula's Good Nutrition Guide for Babies, Toddlers, and Preschoolers: Answers to Parents Most Common Questions Plus Help for Coping with Fussy Eaters by Paula M. Elbirt, MD. Perseus Publishing, 2001
Common sense approaches and excellent reference on nutrition and the fussy eater.

Child of Mine: Feeding with Love and Good Sense by Ellyn Satter.
Bull Publishing Company, 2000
A well written guide on both nutrition and also on how to develop healthy eating habits right from the beginning.

Toilet Training for Two Years or Older

Guide to Toilet Training by The American Academy of Pediatrics, 2003

Mommy! I Have to Go Potty: A Parents Guide to Toilet Training by Jan Faul Raefield. Roberts Publishing, 1996

Toilet Training in Less than a Day by Nathan Azrin. Pocket Books, 1989
Serious behavior modification techniques for children who are ready but resistant.

Once Upon A Potty (Boy and Girl) Versions by Alona Frankel.
Harper-Collins, 1999
Great book for the kids

Toilet Training Without Tears by Charles E. Schaefer. Signet, 1989
Good step-by-step approach, less intense than the 24-hour time frame.

Sleep

PLEASE NOTE: Some publications may have been published before the American Academy of Pediatrics made recommendations on sleep position and may still suggest placing the baby to sleep on his/her stomach. The American Academy of Pediatrics does not recommend this position unless advised by your pediatrician or family practitioner.

Guide to Your Child's Sleep by George J. Cohen, editor. The American Academy of Pediatrics, Villard Books, 1999.
A new book, which hopes to sort out some of the conflicting advice parents receive.

Sleeping Through the Night by Jodi A. Mindell. Harper Perennial, 1997
Well written and offers step by step guides for parents.

Winning Bedtime Battles: How to Help Your Child Develop Good Sleep Habits by Charles E. Schaefer. Citadel Press, 1992
Well written and supports parents in their efforts. Has good sections on older children as well.

Temper Tantrums and Behavior

The Chocolate-Covered-Cookie Tantrum by Deborah Blumenthal. Illustrated by Harvey Stevenson. Clarion Books, 1996
For children, a picture book and story about Sophie's tantrum in the park about a cookie. I liked it as a way to communicate about tantrums to a child who is having a lot of them.

No More Tantrums — A Parent's Guide to Taming Your Toddler and Keeping Cool by Diane Mason. Contemporary Books, 1997
Practical and very popular.

First Aid for Tantrums by Kathy Levinson. Saturn Press, 1997
Good book, easy to read and focuses just on tantrums — what they mean and how to handle them.

When "NO" Gets You Nowhere by Mark L. Brenner. Prima Publishing, 1997
This is also a well-written book aimed at teaching your toddler self control. It is based on the teachings of the late Haim Ginnott who was a pioneer in studying the emotional world of children and our communication with that world.

Fathers

The New Father: A Dad's Guide to the Toddler Years by Armin A. B Rott. Abbeville Press, 1997

VIDEOS

Could You Save Your Child's Life? CPR Review for Infants and Children. American Heart Association Guidelines. Northstar Entertainment, 1999

I Am Your Child hosted by Tom Hanks
Looking at the Critical Importance of parenting skills.

Safety Tech: Making Your Home Safe for Children
Ten Things Every Child Needs

For your convenience many of these links can be accessed from **www.simplyparenting.com.**

General Information

www.AAP.org
The American Academy of Pediatrics Web site. The official place with advice and information about every topic in pediatrics. Many of their books and videos are available on this site.

www.generalpediatrics.com
A website created by a general pediatrician at the University of Iowa which provides a search engine and links to topics on all areas of pediatrics.

www.tnpc.com
The National Parenting Center (800) 753-6667
Reviews of the finest products and services for children and their parents.

www.Kidshealth.org
Wonderful site! **The Nemours Foundation.** Non-Profit dedicated to children's health. Non-commercial. Well-written articles. Easy to use search engine.

Temperament

www.preventiveoz.org
The Preventive Ounce: Creating an Image of Your Child's Temperament. Take the short survey and they will give you an assessment of your toddler's temperament.

www.zerotothree.org
Great article on temperamental traits and how to help your child. Search on Temperament.

Breastfeeding

www.lalecheleague.org
La Leche League International (800) LALECHE

www.breastfeedingonline.com
Information from our experienced Lactation Consultant.

Child Safety

www.aapcc.or
American Association of Poison Control Centers
(800) 222-1222
How to locate your local poison control number.

www.iafcs.org
International Association for Child Safety
(888) 677-IACS
Promoting safety awareness and injury prevention for children.

www.safekids.org
National Safe Kids Campaign (800) 441-1888
National non-profit organization dedicated to the prevention
of unintentional childhood injury.

www.perfectlysafe.com
(800) 837-5437
Child safety products for every room in your house-well
organized catalog of safety items.

www.saferchild.org
Safer Child, Inc.
General child care information and links to other helpful sites.

**Child Passenger
Safety**

www.preventinjury.org/specneeds.asp
Automotive Safety Program
National leader and expert in transportation of children
with special health care needs.

www.nhtsa.dot.gov
National Highway Traffic Safety Administration
(888) DASH2DOT
Information on child passenger safety and car seat inspections.

www.carseat.org
Safety Belt Safe USA (800) 745- SAFE
National, non-profit organization dedicated to child passenger safety.

Medical

www.redcross.org
For information on First Aid and CPR training.

www.vaccines.ashastd.org
CDC National Immunization Information Hotline and
Homepage (American Social Health Association) with
FAQs about immunizations.
(800) 232-2522

Medical	**www.ndss.org** **National Down Syndrome Society** **www.sbaa.org** **Spina Bifida Association of America** (800) 621-3141
Mothers and Fathers	**www.mothersandmore.org** Support for women who interrupted careers to stay home with children. **www.newdads.com** **Boot Camp for New Dads** Offers support and education for men who are preparing to become dads. **www.fathers.com** National Center for Fathering
Special Parenting Situations	**www.mostonline.org** **Mothers of Super Twins (M.O.S.T.)** Support network for families of triplets or more. **www.nomotc.org** **National Organization of Mothers of Twins Clubs (NOMOTC)** Support group for parents of twins and higher order multiple birth. **naic.acf.hhs.gov (no www.)** **National Adoption Information Clearinghouse** Federally-funded one-stop resources for information on all aspects of child adoptions. **www.parentswithoutpartners.org** Organization devoted to the interests of single parents and their children. **www.2moms2dads.com** Offers information and support for gay and lesbian parents.

NOTES